Green Pastures

A childhood at the Gobbins in the 1900s

From the memoirs of Margaret McBride née Welsh

Edited, Illustrated and Produced
by
Pauline E Bingham

Psalm 23: He maketh me to lie down in green pastures,
He leadeth me beside the still waters.

Published in 2014 by Pmacdee Publishing
©2014 Pauline E Bingham

ISBN 978-0-9929220-0-9

First Edition
First Impression

Designed by April Sky Design, Newtownards
www.aprilsky.co.uk

Front/Back Cover: The Gobbins, early summer 2010, showing Woodside's Farm
and the cottages where the Welsh family once lived, close to the Gobbins cliffs.
(Photo by Pauline E. Bingham)

Introduction

About fifteen years ago I found myself working by coincidence with the late Mrs Margaret McBride's grandson, Tom Hamilton. Tom had been the inspiration for Margaret's childhood memories of her life at the Gobbins eventually being put down on paper. He and her granddaughters had often enjoyed listening to these stories at their grandmother's knee. Tom recalled Margaret painstakingly typing out her memoirs with one hand.

As an Islandmagee woman myself, I was most interested to read this unpublished manuscript which Margaret had entitled, 'Green Pastures'. It is a sympathetic and compelling account of a way of life in Islandmagee over a century ago that had nearly disappeared when I was a young girl and in the Millennium does not exist at all.

I was delighted to be given permission by Mrs McBride's family to edit, illustrate and publish 'Green Pastures' for a wider audience to enjoy and I hope that she would approve and be pleased that her 'beloved Gobbins', can again be celebrated. It is particularly relevant now that work is in progress to build a brand new Gobbins Marine Walk, something that I believe Margaret Welsh McBride would also have greatly appreciated.

Pauline E Bingham 2014

Dedication

This book is dedicated to my grandson, Thomas Andrew Hamilton, who inspired me to make the attempt to tell the story of my childhood days at the lovely Gobbins, Islandmagee.

Margaret McBride

> … 'The Gobbins - aye say it softly,
> For my heart is ready to break.
> Its tender childhood memories
> Never will I ever forsake.
> Our little whitewashed cottage
> a stones throw from the sea;
> The Gobbins, unique in its splendour
> Hallowed spot in sweet Islandmagee.
>
> No, no, I cannot tell its beauty,
> So I will put down my pen;
> To our menfolk in their ships,
> I will leave the telling to them.
> Over a broad horizon,
> As their ships go out to the sea,
> In every port hear the whisper:
> "I come from sweet Islandmagee."

(From the poem entitled 'Islandmagee' by Margaret McBride, (Donaldson and Glenn. Pub 1968)

Foreword

To Mrs McBride's original manuscript, written in the late 1960's

'The late Dr Richard Hayward once said that Islandmagee was different to every other part of Ireland. It had a beauty of its own and the people a unique personality of their own, he commented. Mr Victor Glenn, who republished Dixon Donaldson's 'History of Islandmagee', was of the same opinion, as was Donaldson himself.

In 'Green Pastures', Mrs Margaret McBride, born Margaret (Maggie) Welsh at the Gobbins in 1906, brings this difference and personality to life. Writing with great sincerity, she tells the story of her own childhood which was spent just a stones throw from the Gobbins Cliffs.

Her memories of visits by members of the Belfast Naturalists Field Club and other holiday makers who sought the peace and tranquillity of the Gobbins, illustrates a way of life that is, alas, no more. She draws sincere pen pictures of her parents, the members of her family and her neighbours. In short, she tells the story of life in Islandmagee around the days of the First World War.

She tells how people lived in the days when life was slower and quieter than it is now. Their interests had a greater depth of meaning. They shared trouble and sorrow as well as happiness. She gives the impression that the people who live around her and visited her childhood home were all part of a loving family.

Her love for writing has always been very strong. It survived a changing world and she can still look back and record events in her own individual way.

I think the reason this story impressed me was because of the author's very deep sincerity and her high regard for all the people she knew.'

Louis Gilbert, Editor,
Carrickfergus Advertiser and East Antrim Gazette

Acknowledgements

I am most grateful to the family of the late Mrs Margaret McBride for allowing me to edit, illustrate and publish her manuscript, 'Green Pastures'. Margaret's grandson, Tom Hamilton and her daughter, Mrs Doreen Hamilton, have been most supportive and helpful in providing information and photographs.

A sincere thank you to everyone else who helped me in any way with the production of this publication. This includes those Islandmagee folk who were always welcoming when I visited and who were able to provide me with either useful information, photos or postcards for the project.

Also to my husband George for his patience and editing assistance. Finally my thanks to April Sky Design for their advice and assistance with design and publishing.

Pauline E Bingham 2014

Green Pastures

Chapter 1
My Childhood Home

I was born in the year 1906, at the Gobbins in Islandmagee and I have no hesitation in saying that I consider my birthplace to be the loveliest in all of Antrim. In its heyday, during my childhood years, the Gobbins Path attracted endless multitudes of visitors from home and abroad, particularly from England and Scotland.

These tourists would book into local hotels like the Laharna or Henry McNeill's in Larne and then parties of them, often accompanied by a guide, would come on certain days to visit the Gobbins. Arriving at the top of the Gobbins Hill in horse brakes, they then proceeded on foot for the remainder of the journey. No one seemed to mind the narrow twisting cart track, for the lane was indescribably lovely, with rambling whin hills on one side clad in orange bloom from early spring and meadows on the other side where cattle and sheep grazed close to the great Gobbins cliffs. Nearby lay the farmhouse itself and in one of the meadows nestled together were three

'Wise's Eye', an oval gap in the rocks, entrance to the Gobbins Marine Path.

small whitewashed thatched cottages known as 'Burnside', for nearby a burn rippled happily by on its way to the sea below where it was soon welcomed by the mighty waters. At the approach to my home, one had a grand view of Blackhead Lighthouse and the waters of Belfast Lough. Reader, I hope that my pen can adequately describe to you my childhood home. Then, and even until this present day, I have often lifted my heart to God and whispered "thank you", for guiding my parents to make this place their one and only home.

Can you picture a whitewashed house with the thatched roof and gable windows only a fields length from the sea, where we could run down over the hill in a few minutes to the path below and immediately have the most magnificent view of the side face of the great Gobbins cliffs? Cliffs where hundreds of seagulls and many other species of bird nested and where the burn cascaded over high boulders to form a pool before it continued on, underneath a little bridge and hence over shingle and stones to be caressed by the waves.

The Gobbins Path, a lovely marine walk which had opened in 1902, only a few years before my birth, commenced when you entered 'Wise's Eye', a man-made oval hole in the cliff. It was the envy of all seaside resorts and in those times considered to be one of the loveliest in the world. Its uniqueness set it apart with the swelling sea on one hand and the mighty rugged cliffs keeping in formation for the entire cliff walk. Numerous stone or wooden

The first cave to explore was 'Sandy Cave', also known as 'Smugglers Cave'.

stairways ascended or descended from the 'Sandy', or 'Smugglers Cave', as it was sometimes called.

Another stairway and then you were confronted by the famous 'Tubular Bridge', which made one gasp in wonderment and awe. It spanned a wide gulf, with the sea coming sweeping triumphantly below as if endeavoring to overthrow its boundaries. I became so familiar with the paths as a child that I believe I could have walked most of them blindfolded, but the 'Tubular Bridge' defied me. Dearly as I loved its majesty and splendour, it always made me hesitate and tremble. The massive circular steel structure, which served to keep the bridge securely in position, should have reassured me, but instead I imagined the sea reaching up and making me it's prey and I would venture timidly out along the wooden platform then suddenly gather my courage and run with fast beating heart to reach solid ground on the other side. What a glorious sight it was, as if suspended in the air with the sea and cliffs paying homage to it.

I had heard that Mr Berkeley Deane Wise[1], the engineer who designed the cliff walk and from where the name 'Wise's Eye' originated, considered it to be his 'masterpiece'. The steel girders to build the bridges had been made in Belfast and floated out to the Gobbins before being raised and secured into their positions, a few years before I was born. There were more

The 'Tubular Bridge' led out to this 70 feet high basalt dyke known as the 'Man o' War'.

Chief Engineer of the Northern Counties Railway, Berkeley Deane Wise, with his wife Leah, beside the Tubular Bridge on the Gobbins Path that he designed and built in 1902.

On reaching the 'Man o' War' stack, a 1908 extension to the path was planned to take visitors across another bridge and on around the Gobbins cliffs to the 'Seven Sisters' caves. On this postcard c 1902, the planned extension was not yet built and has simply been sketched in. The Belfast Naturalists Field Club Vice President, William J Fennell, is standing in the middle of the 'Tubular Bridge'.

bridges and caves and then came the final one, known as the 'Dark Cave'. It was most intriguing, for you walked in complete darkness for a few minutes then suddenly a ray of light penetrated through and gradually you could see your way ahead again. Next came a swinging suspension bridge, which hung like a great hammock, giving endless fun to children and adults alike. And here the cliff walk came to an end.

" THE RIFT AT THE STYE STEPS, THE GOBBINS NEAR BELFAST."

The Gobbins Marine Walk was only partially extended to Wise's original plans in 1908. The 'Stye Steps' brought visitors out of a tunnel blasted through the basalt below sea level and then returned to the cliff path. This led on to the 'Otter Cave' and by suspension bridge across 'Gordon's Leap'.

From 'Otter Cave', a spectacular 250ft Suspension Bridge led across 'Gordon's Leap', bridging the mouths of six of the 'Seven Sisters' caves, where the Gobbins Marine Walk came to an end. Visitors then had to retrace their path to 'Wise's Eye'.

My Gobbins home was humble and poor, but what it lacked in luxury it made up for greatly in love and understanding, as I hope you will agree as my story unfolds. It consisted of a kitchen and a small pantry as you entered the porch on the left, where a little window overlooked the field leading to the cliffs. A brown sink with a water tap from which a pipe was attached ran into a rain water barrel outside. We had to carry fresh water daily from the meadow a fields length away. A wooden working bench scrubbed white held water buckets and saucepans underneath it. The walls were painted with red distemper and a shelf right round the entire pantry held over a dozen or more teapots in various sizes of china, delph and enamel. Mother catered for the tourists and visitors to the Gobbins in the summer, indeed from early spring onwards. Our kitchen had a big wide fireplace with hobs on either side and the big iron kettle, mostly always on the boil, hung by a crook attached to an iron crane. The hearth was whitewashed and a steel fender, a double mantel-board stacked with various things: ornaments, photo frames, vases, two china dogs and a bicycle lamp or two completed the fireplace. Two scrubbed tables with stools below, an old well-worn leather couch, father's old wooden arm chair, a big cupboard with a top half of glass doors; then a homemade stand placed against a door leading into our tea room, held lots of cups, saucers, plates etc. This was always removed when the visiting season began, giving more access into the tea room. The cottage's cement floor had many cracks on it and a homemade rag rug sat before the hearth. A tiny room off the kitchen held only a bed, a small wash stand and a chair. A step ladder served as the stairway to the loft above which my father had boarded in so it looked like proper stairs. There were three double beds in the loft where a long rounded wooden beam stretched across the room. I think it served to make the ceiling stronger. A candlestick had been placed in the centre and we children were warned repeatedly by our parents to be careful not to tamper with it, for it would take very little to set the thatched roof on fire. I loved the bed facing the window in the gable and from early summer especially I would make the greatest effort to get sleeping in it, for it was sheer delight to lie in the evenings before sleep overcame me and feast on the lovely scenery, watching the boats sail past the Gobbins Head or glimpse rabbits and hares capering about the field. If I listened intently and no-one disturbed me, I could actually hear the delightful song of the burn.

My parents had a family of seven living and two more had not survived

Welsh's Cottage and Tearooms at the Gobbins. Dixon Donaldson, who wrote the 'History of Islandmagee' in 1927, is sitting at the table on the right.

birth. I had two brothers and four sisters and was the fifth one in the family, considered the only delicate one. I was slight and thin and had inherited my father's pale complexion. Mollie, two years my junior, was plump and had lovely rosy cheeks. People would ask my mother what ailed me. "Will you ever rear her? " they would ask. "She could eat a man off his horse! " mother would retort. My eldest sister Nellie worked in Turner's Fruit Shop in Belfast and another, Aggie, was a nursemaid in a gentleman's house in the city too. They came home some weekends. My brothers Jim and Davie, in their early teens, worked to some of the big farmers in Islandmagee. I knew there was always a pang in my mother's heart when she thought of her boys, for the time would eventually come when they would follow the tradition of most Island men and choose to go to sea. Islandmagee was known the world over as a seafaring community.

I have always considered my mother a lovely looking woman and none of her daughters excelled her in looks. She was blue eyed with a fine open face. Tall and slim with a waist as neat as any young girl and with the loveliest auburn hair that seemed somehow to sparkle with vitality and which she always wore coiled on top of her head. She possessed the nice soft clear complexion usually associated with a redhead. At the time my story begins she had scarcely a grey hair, despite her fortyfour years or so. My mother had a cheery, optimistic outlook on life and dear knows she had not often much to be cheery about, for life in those days was very hard. She enjoyed sharing a joke with most people and such a hearty laugh she had. Mother had a permanent bad leg, a 'white swelling'[2], the doctor termed it, which had developed after the birth of her first child. The doctor told her it would go away after the birth of another child, but baby after baby had arrived and the swelling did not improve. She was forced to wear a boot belonging to my father and cut it further open to allow her foot to squeeze in. The top of the foot was also swollen and her leg very thick right up to the knee. Fortunately in those days, long clothes were the fashion. But mother was not afraid to have a laugh with others about her leg. I remember once she raised her skirts and with a solemn expression asked some visitors, "Do you think I should join our local football team?" My father David Welsh, two years her senior, was of slim build with a pale complexion and little moustache. Of my parents he was the more quiet and reserved, quite happy and contented to let my mother take the helm. His people came from Loughmourne near Carrickfergus and he was one of a large family. Mother was an Islandmagee woman and herself one of a family of sixteen.

I have left the cream of the milk, as it were, to the last. My youngest sister Beatrice, then still a baby in arms, was the pick of the bunch and we all just idolised her, particularly my two brothers Jim and Davie. However, as my story unfolds, you will read how another baby also came to be part of our family.

Chapter 2
Winter Fuel

Looking back over my childhood years, I can remember the following events so well that even to this day, I can recall them almost word for word. I was about eleven years of age and our youngest sister Beatrice was just beginning to toddle about. For a change, Mollie and I were occupying the room off the kitchen. Being a light sleeper at all times, I had wakened early on this bright autumn morning. I could see the blue skies through the window that looked over the lovely winding lane I have mentioned. Mollie was still fast asleep, with one plait of her hair softly caressing a rosy cheek. I could hear mother getting father's breakfast ready, as the clock on the wall below struck seven. I knew the routine every morning, mother would go and let the hens out when the kettle was put on the boil, then Belinda the old brown hen would come clucking in. She might have been very old, but she ruled all the other hens and the saucy roosters as well. They were no match for her impertinence. If mother was a few minutes late in letting her out she would make a fuss flying round and round in a circle with her wings outstretched. "Stick her in the pot and make a good pot of soup," father would comment. "Soup, it would taste like glue," mother laughed, "and she might fly up and confront us all. No, Belinda remains, because she really is a pet, and we should have respect for her old age." So Belinda would come clucking in, picking up stray crumbs. She would be followed by her mate Snowball, a grey and white cat who was a terrific hunter. Rabbits and hares alike were her prey. Yet despite this talent, our father, who did not like cats, was not keen on Snowball. Sensing his disapproval, she would stay underneath the table until he left for work.

"It was a terrible night's rain, Davie. I thought the heavens had opened." "I never heard a thing. Surely it was not all that bad, Aggie?" "Well, go out and have a look round the corner of the house. The burn has overflowed and Woodside's and Tom Browne's fields are flooded. It is judgement weather. Your egg is ready and I am putting no cheese in your lunch box. It is too hard to digest. I put a farl of yellowmeal bread in for you and one for Ned Jones[1]. Martha Strahan[2] got a bag of it in yesterday." "Good for you, Aggie. I wouldn't mind a good bowl of yellow meal porridge for my dinner tonight, seeing my stomach is out of order." "I will send the wee girls to Marriott Holmes'[3] for an extra pint of milk. Buttermilk is too sour. I'm expecting Sam Duff with coal today, though I don't believe a quarter will do us until Christmas." "Keep the wee girls off school today and get them to bring a lot of whin runts down from the whin hill." "Now, is that not like a man. You never use an ounce of common sense. Sure you know the whin hill will be soaking wet after last nights deluge. Another thing, the School Attendance Inspector[4] is due in school any day. I don't want him on my tails." "Well, if it should dry up and you decide to go, be sure to put on your elastic bandage. You know what happened last time with the ugly scratch you got."

I sat up in bed gasping with excitement. Oh, what a chance to escape school for a day. I thought of my unfinished exercise. I was supposed to draw the glass vase on my teacher's desk as part of my homework. I could not draw the base, let alone the nickeled stem. But Jamie Kane[5] from Mullaghdoo, now his would be a work of art! It was always put on the blackboard for the class to view. Mine would be hideous and no sane person could call it a vase. Mollie had already hers done and it was extra good. "No, I've done my own drawing," was her reply when I asked her to help me. Why had girls to do drawing at all, I thought. What possible use could it be to one in later life? And then there was my horrible school bag. Mother had made it out of a bit of grey canvas - secretly I thought it was a big, ugly contraption. "Oh, look at Maggie Welsh's new school bag," John Macaulay[6] had shouted. "It's like a horse's nose bag! " All my fellow scholars had tittered and teased

Kilcoan, Islandmagee.

Kilcoan Limestone Quarry, Islandmagee was worked in the late 19th and early 20th century. Directly across Larne Lough, was Ballylig Quarry at Magheramorne, where Maggie's father Davie Welsh worked as a labourer.

me. I had shed bitter tears and although Mr Tom Douther our schoolmaster, had come on the scene and sternly reprimanded them, I wasn't convinced that the episode was finished with.

Soon I heard mother saying cheerio to father and the sound of his bicycle wheeling out through the bullocks gate. He would have to walk along most of the lane until he came to the Back Road, as it was called then. Father worked at the Ballylig Limestone Quarries[7] near Magheramorne, quite a considerable distance away. It was hard work and the pay very poor, especially in the winter time when there were many weeks broken pay when he earned only a few shillings.

I lay in bed listening to mother's movements. She was brushing the floor, then she would lift the ashes and whitewash the hearth and maybe give the fender a rub. "Snowball, watch that boiling kettle. Do you want to be scalded?" I smiled. Snowball would always attempt to lie the full length of the fender. I could hear Beatrice, who was just beginning to walk, scrambling down the stairs. She would be picked up and hugged and a lot of childish prattle would follow.Then mother started to sing. This meant she was putting on her clothes.

"If I come to Jesus, He will make me glad,
He will give me pleasure when my heart is sad.
If I come to Jesus, happy shall I be
He is gently calling little ones like me."

Mother had a fine singing voice and was often asked for a verse. Her singing finished, mother came into our room. She whirled the bed clothes to the bottom of the bed. "Up, girls, up." Mollie rubbed her eyes with annoyance and tried to cover herself up again. I told mother that I had heard her conversation with father. "So please let us go to the whin hill today." I pleaded eagerly. "Your ears are too long my girl. I have a good mind to make you sleep upstairs again. Goodness knows you fight enough to get sleeping upstairs in summer. No, it is school today for you both." Mollie sat suddenly up in bed. "Please mother, we will work like slaves all day." "Such unbounded energy," laughed mother. "No, the hill will be far too wet and messy to work in." "But mother, look, there is the sun actually coming out and it will soon dry up, besides we can both put on our oldest clothes." We both pleaded away and eventually mother gave in. "But remember, it will be hard work all day girls!"

In an hour, after a hurried breakfast of wheaten porridge and tea, we were on our way. Mollie had put Beatrice into the old 'perambulator', with a bottle of milk and bread and an old teddy bear. We left her in a safe position in the field where she could look up and see us. Mother carried a saw and a hatchet and we carried ropes.

Halfway up the whin hill, I stopped to gaze at the scene before me. From early childhood I have been a keen admirer of nature. I have quite honestly throughout my life, never awoken in the morning without being thrilled at the dawn of another day. Of course some days have brought with them sorrow, tragedy and even death, as is the lot of all mankind. But as regards nature, there is something spiritual and majestic in the birth of a new day. Night, with its approaching shadows, also has its own beauty. The seasons each in their turn have their own superb beauty also. A rainbow in the sky has never failed to fill me with wonderment and made me appreciate how faithful and trustworthy God's spoken word is. The moonlight flooding the earth in harvest has made me look on in awe and worship. But my greatest inspiration is in the wild, rugged, unkempt beauty of nature untouched and untamed by the hand of man. The majestic clifftops of my beloved

The majestic Gobbins Head.

Gobbins stood aloof in their own singular beauty. I have never been impressed with blue seas and miles of golden sands or man's attempts to modernise the seaside with the latest devices. The artificial look of it all has no appeal for me.

Today, in the mellow October sunshine, our surroundings were breath-takingly lovely. A John Kelly's coal boat had just entered Belfast Lough round the bend of the cliffs. It was sailing so close I could just make out the tiny figures of some of her crew on deck as she headed towards port. A slight breeze had sprung up and the row of trees behind our house were swaying gently. Their lovely tinted leaves fell so slowly down as if reluctant to say farewell. The old hawthorn tree that grew just outside our porch door and spread its branches to almost completely cover our thatched roof, was poorly clad now. It had been so lovely all summer, contrasting delightfully with the whitewashed cottage. Many visitors had stopped to admire it and to take snaps and whenever possible customers would have a meal or cup of tea seated in its shade. Mollie and I loved to clamber over it's branches and had carved our initials into the bark. On this particular morning a great yearning stole over me. I wanted right then to be able to pay a tribute to my wonderful Gobbins, some way or somehow. There might never be a song in praise of it! Little did I think then that later in my life, the poem I had written in tribute would appear in the 'History of Islandmagee'[8] and thus be handed down to posterity.

I could see that the burn had overflowed its banks with the heavy incessant rain. A thick plank that served as a bridge at one point where we crossed it to reach the farm was almost completely submerged by the raging torrent. But it was gradually receding now. There seemed to be a lot of activity going on at Robert John Woodside's farm. A farm servant was driving a herd of cattle out into the raindrenched meadow. Robert Woodside had a big farm and

Woodside's Farm at the Gobbins and on left 'Burnside Cottages' in 2010.

owned a lot of land. His wife had died some years back. John, one of his sons, was stalking over the field to the Gobbin Head with a couple of collie dogs at his heels. He was probably going to look at his fence, as father said they had lost a valuable cow over the cliffs the previous evening. I was sure that was his daughter, Mary, hanging out a big washing in the stackyard. She was taking advantage of the dry weather. The turkeys had been let out into the same field and I could distinctly hear the gobbles of an old gander over the roar of the burn. Between our home and their farm was of course the 'Burnside Cottages', which belonged to the Woodsides. What nice families had lived in them all summer. In fact, some of them had been coming year after year. Mollie and I had made friends with some of the children, who rarely had to be reprimanded about swinging on the gates or damaging the farmers' crops.

A Mrs Foote and her delicate daughter had occupied one of them for several years now. Florence had a weak chest and was pale and wan. Mother took her under her wing and supplied her with baked bread and had kept Daisy's milk mostly for her. Daisy was our goat and you will hear more about her presently. At first Florence had shuddered at drinking goats milk, but mother was firm. "It will stick to your ribs dear and bring health back to you," and sure enough Florence improved. A lump of earth skimmed my ankles. "Come on Maggie Welsh, don't expect me to do your work," Mollie yelled from above me. I turned to obey, but then I hesitated, for there was Daisy peeping at me over a whin bush. Last week she had tossed me into the ditch and butted me. I knew she disliked me much more than Mollie, but she loved Mother and would allow only her to take her milk. "She won't touch you," called mother. Daisy was nibbling the bush and evidently enjoying it. "Touch her indeed," she seemed to be saying, "I have no intention, at least not this morning." Just at that moment the postman's welcome whistle greeted us. Quick as lightening Mollie came bounding down past me, pushing me aside to run as fast as her legs would carry her. She ran up over the rough uneven path to the left of the stile at the foot of Aggie Johnston's Brae. Here the postman Alfie Jackson[9] had left the letter in a rabbit's hole. "It is from Aggie and Nellie," she called out, having recognised the writing.

Mrs David Welsh
The Gobbins
Islandmagee
Co Antrim

Mother read out the letter to us. The main news was that our sisters had joined the Iron Mission Hall Church[10] in Belfast. This was very pleasing to mother. "Thank God for that girls, you know that there are many temptations in town for young people." Two one pound notes nestled in the envelope.

"God love them," said mother tenderly." "Their wages are little enough and Nellie has to pay for her board and lodging. Isn't God good, girls. His love and mercy never fails. This extra bit of money should get us an extra four bags of coal, pay two weeks rent and buy a bag of cut corn for the hens. There might even be enough to get some sock wool!"

We worked hard all morning with only a short break for something to eat. We would saw or chop off the whin heads, then saw them into lengths. Mother knew how to tie up each bundle of sticks, then making sure that the path below was clear we would all give a push and the bundles would go bouncing down over the hill without a stick scarcely out of place. Our brothers could help us at the weekend to trail them down the field to the coalshed. Beatrice had a long sleep in the afternoon as we worked away, then Sam Duff came with the coal. "Watch out, Sam!" mother called down to him as a big bundle of whin runts came bounding down just behind his cart. "Boy, oh boy, Mrs Welsh, I would need to take out an insurance policy before coming here! Hello Mollie," he said as he spotted her. "When are you coming to keep house for me?" "What about Maggie, would she not suit you?" mother shouted down. "Oh, Mollie is my sort of good looker and a worker into the bargain." Mollie's face went bright red. I stuck my tongue out at him from behind a bush. As he talked to my mother in the loudest tones possible, Mollie and I were giggling on the side at him. Sam was interesting but he seemed ancient to us and no-one knew how old he really was. My father said he was over seventy, his green battered hat pulled down over his forehead with wisps of grey locks peeping out behind his ears and a short thick neck. His trousers were always an intriguing feature, for they appeared miles too wide for him. The story around Islandmagee was that on more that one occasion Sam's trousers had slipped down before he became aware of it. Tottie, his pony, was a beautiful creature. She was a lovely pearl grey, quite elegant and stepped out so gracefully, far too refined, in my opinion, to be engaged in the coal industry. Bessie, his mongrel bitch was much more suited to the profession. She was black as coal, with only one white spot on her breast and always travelled on top of the dirty old coal bags. I thought she couldn't be very comfortable, for as well as the hard coals, Sam's old cart was almost falling to pieces. "You know where to put the coals, Sam. If I stopped now the work would never go on." "Right, Mrs Welsh," he shouted in his wheezy voice. "Oh and Sam, I left you a shilling for yourself and the teapot is warm on the hob. You'll find a farl of sweet soda on the table." "Thank you kindly. I see you had a wee bit of a flood last night." "I'll give you a wee bit of a flood indeed," retorted mother. "Was it not bad with you then, Sam?" "Not at all. I had a bit of an Indian summer all night," Sam laughed heartily. "No, it was bad Mrs Welsh, the rain came down like a water spout. I had to shift my bed to the far gable."

"You are a foolish old miser, Sam. What good is your money if you do not enjoy it. It is about time you moved out of that old tin hut and at least got a decent wee cottage." "You're a wise woman Mrs Welsh, I will do what you suggest when I find an old girl with a nest egg."

When Sam moved on, Mother turned on us sternly. "I could have boxed your ears! Have a bit of respect, girls. Let me tell you this, old Sam may be an unusual character, but in the next generation his sort will be extinct and the world will be a less interesting place."

Thus rebuked, we worked hard until it was time to go back and prepare father's dinner, ready for his return from work. Tonight he was only having porridge, but we were having potatoes mashed with raw onion, some butter and a glass of buttermilk. Mollie, for some reason, was in the best of spirits, perhaps because of the compliment paid to her today by the opposite sex, for she even offered to do the drawing exercise of the deplorable vase for me. We were in bed long before eight o'clock and for once I was asleep almost before my head touched the pillow.

Chapter 3
The Poem

Mollie and I were worried. This morning our mother was acting very strangely and seemed absentminded. She had not even put on Beattie's clothes and her little ladyship was sitting on the floor making havoc with the sock wool. Furthermore, it was now a quarter to nine and Daisy had not been milked and she was always milked on the dot every morning. Mother was muttering to herself, a sure sign that something was in the wind. Had something happened last night when we were asleep? Oh if only I had not gone to sleep. Our concerns were not to be satisfied however, for suddenly mother gave a start. "Dear dear, I am woolgathering this morning. Come on girls, it's time you were away to school." "Has anything happened mother, that we don't know about?" I braced myself to ask. "Happened, what could have happened since last night?" she retorted sharply. "Look here Maggie, I am going to make you and Mollie sleep upstairs after this, for I do declare that you both do nothing but eavesdrop every night. Curiosity you remember is a vice, you wee devil." She snatched the wool away from Beattie and smacked her hand. "Did none of you see her at my wool?" Reluctantly I slipped my

Hillsport and the Gobbins.

Hill's cottage situated top left near the Gobbins cliffs.

ugly old schoolbag over my shoulder and followed Mollie out the door.

At the stile I stopped for a moment before proceeding up over Johnston's Brae. Mollie had gone on ahead; she loved company and would be calling first for Robert and John Kane and then further on down the Lang Dale, Jeannie, Mollie and Hugh Caldwell[1] would probably be waiting for her. It was called the Lang Dale because the path wound a long way before it came to the main road. It was a good fresh morning. The tide was full in and Johnny Hill was out tethering his two goats.

The Hills[2] lived down below us, almost at the waters edge. Mother said that even before I was born in 1906, the Hills had been the best of friends with them, going in and out of each other's houses. There were two Hill sons married and two young daughters had died in the bloom of womanhood. Mrs Maggie Hill was an invalid and confined indoors. She could only move around a little. Her only outing was when Johnny took her in his horse and trap about once a week up the rocky uneven path past our house to the main road. The Hills had adopted an orphan girl called Annie who was now old enough to manage their tea rooms for them. Hill's teahouse lay over in one of their fields a little way from their house, a low red painted hut with a sign painted in big white letters, 'Hill's Tea Rooms'. Their business had existed before my parents had started up in opposition. It was this rivalry that had put paid to their friendship.

View from Gobbins to Blackhead.

The rugged Gobbins shoreline. Hill's Cottage and their Tearooms can be seen above right.

"But there is enough business for us both," my mother had pleaded. "What with the English and Scotch tourists and Irish visitors. Why, the Gobbins is getting more popular every year." But the Hills had turned a deaf ear. "Well, my mother said finally, "I find that I have to do something to supplement my income and the tea making is the only alternative." All her pleading had come to nothing. She could carry on with her scheme if she wished, but their friendship was at an end. Mother had not her red hair for nothing. She told us that she had let fly with her tongue and flounced out of their house, never to enter it again. The next day she had gone as usual to the well for water. But Johnny Hill was waiting for her and ordered her to never dare come near the well again. She stood up to him, threatening to throw a bucket of water round him if he spoke further. She got her way at the time, but when she returned later to the well Johnny had filled it in. They had another spring in their garden. She told us that she could feel their eyes burning into her back as she returned home angrily with her empty pail.

Luckily father soon found another source of water in the field opposite Burnside. He was not a professional water diviner, but it was said of him that he could lure water out of a stone. With the boys helping him at the weekend, they faced the new well. There were actually two other wells in Tom Browne's fields but there the water was too soft for good tea. The one at Hill's had been pure spring water.

I had a good half hours walk or more to attend Mullaghdoo School[3]. It was on the main Upper Road (Middle Road) about a mile from Ballycarry Station with a few more into Whitehead. I had just time to hurry into school before Mr and Mrs Douther,[4] our headmaster and his wife, arrived in their small new car. Until recently they had travelled by pony and trap. We pupils knew with a glance at our master that he was in bad form today, for a strand of stray hair had fallen unnoticed over his brow. This stray wisp of hair was a bad sign. It never failed to put us on the alert. Thomas Douther was a big powerful man, everything about him denoting strength. He walked with purposeful steps. I think he was then a little over forty years old, with his wife Annie a few years younger. She was the sister of our landlord, Tom Browne of the Gobbins. Tall and tiny waisted, she wore her fair hair on top of her head in a bun. She had a lovely pink complexion and wore the prettiest frilly blouses with long skirts, with a narrow black velvet choker always around her slender throat.

There was a good attendance at Mullaghdoo school this particular day. The number written on the blackboard stated eighty-nine. My class settled down to work, quiet as lambs, although inwardly we were concerned about that stray strand of hair. This was the senior class, but Mrs Douther was taking it for some reason. Not that this made much difference, as both were stern and took no nonsense. The two classrooms were divided by a wooden

Mullaghdoo(dubh) National School c 1910. On right, Mr Thomas Douther the Master and Mrs Douther assistant teacher on left.
Back Row: James Heggan, Sam Picken, Joe Mann, Margaret Aiken, Minnie Alexander, Sarah Alexander, Margaret Allen, ... , Martha Strahan
3rd Row: Joe Weatherall, Douglas Orr, Lizzie Henderson, Mary Henderson, Mabel Orr, William J Heggan, John Henderson, John Strahan, ... McLarnon,
2nd Row: Jean Heggan, Mollie Duff, Martha Wilson, Maud Strahan, Nellie Mann, James Duffy, Billy McGrady, Dan Heggan, Margaret Duffy
1st Row: Agnes Mann, Tom Heggan, ... Davidson, Peggy Orr, Lily Cameron, Margaret Cameron, WJ Heggan, Tom Mann, Samuel H Duff

partition, the top half of it glass. Mrs Douther was sitting at a small table going over papers and letters when she gasped and every head turned in her direction. She clutched a sheet of blue writing paper and her cheeks flushed a deep pink." Who wrote this ghastly rubbish?" she demanded in a loud, sharp voice. Every eye suddenly turned to me. The class had a shrewd idea that it might be one of my wonderful poems that I was always bragging about. "Maggie Welsh. Is this your work?" I hung my head in assent.

"Read it out to the class. Do as I say! " she commanded. I had no alternative but to obey.

This story I am going to tell
No doubt it will seem to rhyme very well
About one particular boy I know
Who teases the girls wherever they go.
Herby Lynas told me a yarn
He flirted with Mollie Welsh in the barn
He kissed and cuddled her in the chaff
Oh what a tale, oh what a laugh,
We have a teacher, the haughty Ann
And her husband the brutal Tam.
If her cheeks flush to deeper red
We pupils would be better dead.
If on Tam's forehead a wisp of hair
Oh scholars I beg you to beware.

The class roared with laughter but stopped short when they saw the thunderous expression on Mrs Douther's face. I stole a quick glance at Mollie, who was in tears. I knew full well I would have to face the consequences from her as well as from my teachers.

My teacher tore the paper into shreds. "Rubbish and trash of the lowest degree! I am surprised at your mother, Maggie Welsh, allowing you so much free time. You would be better employed doing your work. You will stay behind after school and I will give you several objects to draw and the work must be perfect. Now, come with me to the master. The rest of you get on with your work. I can see a firmer hand is required here in future."

Weeping, I was brought to the master for my punishment. He showed no mercy. His strap fell across my legs and knuckles and soon my hands were red and bleeding. I returned to class in agony. My legs were stiff and I felt as if I had fallen into a bed of nettles. It was sheer agony to grip my pen. No one dared to look at me, bent industriously over their desks.

I was sure it was Herby Lynas, the sneak, who had betrayed me. Herbie was the young farm hand who worked for Mrs Browne and her son Tom

The original old school bell of Mullaghdubh Primary School, on the school wall in 2012.

and of course Mrs Douther was also Mrs Browne's daughter. Herby had a notion of Mollie and I was jealous. Indeed I was doubly jealous when Herby's chum, Sammy Hawthorn of the Back Road, also seemed taken with Mollie, leaving me ignored and the odd one out on almost every occasion. Yes, I remembered Herbie trying to snatch the poem from me as I sat at the roadside waiting for Mercer the Baker's[5] breadcart a few days ago. Then I had hinted at its contents. "I am glad," I thought to myself defiantly, "It is worth all the pain I am going to suffer to know that the whole class now knows about the affair in Marriott's barn."

Half an hour later the school inspector's arrival occasioned Mrs Douther to go into the other classroom with him. The entire class breathed a sigh of relief. But the atmosphere seemed to be one of defiance now. There was scarcely a docile pupil. Jamie Niblock[6], a palefaced boy, got to his feet. He was a bit of 'a devil', always bent on mischief. "If I go and put the clock on a wee bit, will you all promise not to tell on me?" he asked. "Quick, they may be back soon." "Yes, yes," every hand shot up in approval, including my own. "Right, and remember, no betrayal." He moved quickly over to the clock which hung above the fireplace, while we watched breathlessly. He opened the front and moved the hands on. "Oh", someone cried, "you have put it too far, she'll notice!" James only just made it back to his seat before Mrs Douther returned. The clock was now over half an hour fast. No pupil dared say a word to give the show away. We worked away as if we loved it. The clock striking the hour caused Mrs Douther to look up. A puzzled expression stole onto her face. Her forehead puckered and again she looked at the clock. For the second time that morning her cheeks flushed and she suddenly marched to the door and opening it beckoned to the master. They spoke in whispers for a moment and then the master thundered "Who touched the clock?" It was a terrible question requiring a terrible answer. But utter silence reigned. "Very well, as everyone is dumb, the strap is the only answer. I will thrash you all individually, seeing you are intent on shielding the culprit." At first no one spoke. Then Jamie Niblock put up his hand. "I moved the clock, sir. It was only for a bit of fun," he said pleadingly. "I might have known it, James Niblock. You are the ringleader in every disgraceful affair and a bad influence on all the other scholars. Come with me." Mr Douther beckoned with his finger. Amazingly, I noticed a slight smile on Jamie's face as he left the room and even when he returned after his severe punishment, he showed no signs of distress.

I was glad that my detention meant Mollie had gone on home earlier. I would at least escape having my hair pulled for disgracing her in class. By now she would have told mother everything, of course, and mother would undoubtedly give me a lecture, but I could visualise the smile lurking behind my dear mother's eyes, for she would likely see the funny side of it. Later, when we sat together in detention, Jamie Niblock whispered, "You will hardly write any more poems now." "Not write any more poems," I gasped. "Of course I will, but I won't write about people. I will devote my talent to only Nature," I said proudly. "God's creation is more interesting than human beings." "Sometimes they are not human." Jamie said, with a nod towards the other room. "Well, I'm going to have a smoke and to hell with the human race!" He brought the butt of a cigarette out from his pocket. I was horrified. Supposing he was caught in the act. But Jamie took an occasional puff as he tried to do the work we had been set. It was hard not to admire that boyish, defiant spirit.

Chapter 4
Wee John Kane

The night was calm and the murmur of the sea was pleasant as it gently ebbed over the stones and shingle. There was a nip in the air with a hint of frost, but it was still pleasant for walking. The night sky was studded with stars and the frequent flashing rays from Blackhead lighthouse lit up our path. Mother walked a little ahead of me, for the path was narrow on the low shore. I knew she was busy with her thoughts and did not feel inclined to chat. This suited my mood well, for even at night I was conscious of the beauty around me and was contemplating how lovely this path by the sea was in all seasons. It was a favourite walk for our family, winding along the coast past Blackhead and finishing at Whitehead.

The coastal path ran northwards from the Gobbins to Whitehead.

Many visitors arriving by train at Whitehead followed this same walk to reach the Gobbins Path. Blackhead had its own singular beauty with caves, a few bridges and a lovely walk round the lighthouse. Then came the Cove, with its rock formations, grassy slopes and a spring diving board stretching out to sea for keener swimmers. It was a popular spot at holiday times and a regatta was held here every summer. The Cove Regatta[1] offered all kinds of boat racing, greasy pole competitions, fancy dress parades, children's sports and of course a popular local band would attend to provide entertainment. The 'fifty-two steps', part of the path built by the Railway company a little further on, were a great delight to us children. We would race up and down these steps like young hares. The path occasionally would leave the waters edge and wind inland a bit over green grass as soft as velvet. The hills above were especially lovely in autumn, covered with blackberries, hips and haws and black sloe trees. A few more ditches and stiles to cross and then round the bend - the breathtaking sight of the majestic Gobbins cliffs.

ISLANDMAGEE DEVELOPMENT & RECREATION SOCIETY

Annual Regatta
(WEATHER PERMITTING), AT

THE COVE,

Saturday, 22nd August, 1925,
At 3-30 p.m. sharp.

Officer of the Day : CAPT. JOHN NIBLOCK.

Judges : CAPTAINS JOHNSTON, AIKEN, KANE, FERGUSON, and Messrs. JOHN ALLEN DUFF, J. NIBLOCK, A. H. DAVISON, M. CHARLESSON, W. CROWE, S. HALL, T. JENKINS and R. CLEMENTS LYTTLE, J.P.

Starter : Mr. R. DICK.

PROGRAMME OF EVENTS.

70 yards Swimming Race for Members of Clubs affiliated to Irish Amateur Swimming Association.

Two Oared Rowing Race for Boats 14 feet and under (Open to all Comers).

Confined to Islandmagee, North of a Line drawn from Blackhead Lighthouse to Slaughterford Bridge.

SWIMMING	ROWING
(Under Irish Amateur Swimming Association Laws.)	1.—Pettel Race (Handicap) for Boys under 16 years.
1.—Diving.	2.—Two Oar Championship Race (Boats 14 feet and under) for Hawkins' Cup and Medals.
2.—Boys (under 16 years) Handicap Race (25 yards).	3.—Two Oar Race (Handicap) for Boys under 16 years.
	4.—Pettel Race (Open).
3.—50 yards (Open).	5.—Two Oar Race (Ladies).
4.—40 yards (Open) Ladies.	6.—Shovel Race.

Entries will be accepted up to 6 p.m. on 19th inst. and further particulars obtained from the Boat Race Committee—J. Leighton, John Mann, J. Niblock, W. J. Stewart, Captains Kane and Ferguson, or W. J. Hawkins, Gobbins Stores, Islandmagee.

Musical Selections by Edenderry Brass and Reed (Prize) Band, 3-30 p.m. to 5-30 p.m., and 7-0 p.m. to 9-0 p.m.

ENTRANCE FEES (each event)—LADIES, 1/6.   BOYS, 1/-.   MEN, 2/-.

VALUABLE PRIZES. (No Third Prize unless 5 Starters).

R. CARSWELL & SON, LTD., Printers, Queen Street, Belfast.

Poster advertising the Cove Regatta, held annually in the 1920's and 30's.

Our destination tonight was a home lying close to the fifty-two steps. As we passed by the Hill's house their blinds were shut, but a Tilly lamp² shone brightly, reflecting the shadow of a flowerpot inside onto the blind. Their dog barked as we passed by. "I wonder what the Hills would say if they knew my mission tonight!" mother said as I followed her over a stile. "But if things go as I hope, they will know soon enough." "Will you be disappointed if Jack says no, Mother?" "Indeed I will, for I have my heart set on the wee darling, especially seeing it is a wee boy. You're a queer one Maggie. You don't seem half as excited as your sister Mollie." "But I am excited Mother. A baby in the house would be very interesting."

As we quickened our steps I thought over the events of the day. When we arrived home from school, Mother had dropped her bombshell. "I've had something on my mind these last few days that we need to talk about, girls." "Ha, retorted Mollie, you can say that again, all that muttering." Mother had laughed. "Well, I had an important decision to make and as it concerns us all it required a lot of thought. I am going to Jack Kane's tonight to ask him if I can look after his baby, and I hope that I may get the child for good." This news astounded us both. Mollie began to dance around with excitement. "A wee baby coming here," she gasped. "Now, now, we will have to wait and see first. Your father told me that Jack Kane had to leave his boat last week to come home and look after the baby." "Yes," I said. "At school Robert Kane told us his Granny Kane was ill." "And you never thought to tell me?" Mother frowned. "It is no joke to have to leave your boat when you run the risk of not getting it back again and it is worse for a wee helpless infant bereft of a mother's love within a few weeks, and an old grandparent not able to cope. Thank God the poor darling's mother passed away the way she did, unaware of what was happening. Can you imagine anything so tragic as a mother knowing that she is leaving her children to the mercy of the world, for even the best of fathers can be so helpless in such a crisis." The tears had trickled down her face, for my mother adored babies and was in her element if any visitor left their baby with her until they returned from walking at the Gobbins. The request to leave them was seldom refused. I expect that they knew to look at her face that they could trust her, and so did the babies, for they hardly ever cried.

"I am taking Maggie with me tonight. She can help carry the clothes if I get him." Mollie was livid. She wanted to go instead of me. "No Mollie, I want a nice dinner for your father to have him in good tune. You make a better cook than Maggie." "I totally disagree Mother," I answered hotly, "just because I like writing does not mean I can do nothing else!" Mother smiled. "Let's not argue about it now. Mollie will look after the house this time. I have not told your father yet of my intentions. He will probably digest it over dinner or as he sits at the fireside. He will be in late for he has to go to

The coastal area running south from the Gobbins to Cloughfin was known as 'the Heughs', meaning steep cliffs or precipice in Old English. The 'fiftytwo steps' went past Jack Kane's house (in centre) and led down to the beach, on bottom left.

Archie Forde's[3] to finish a kitchen cabinet. Stick Beattie up to bed at seven and keep a good fire on."

Molly had to give in with good grace and mother and I left the house that evening about half past six. Kane's house lay near the 'fifty-two steps', in a sheltered spot with the whin brae behind it. Locals called the area 'The Heughs',[4] because of its many crags and cliffs. Rupert, their old sheepdog, came barking and sniffing around us as we approached. The door opened and Jack Kane himself stood framed in the doorway by the light streaming out into the night. "Rupert, here boy," he called, peering out. "Hello Jack. Don't be alarmed, its not robbers," mother called out brightly. "Oh Aggie, it's you. Right glad I am to see you and hear your voice. Come on right in. I see you have got one of your wee lassies with you. Take a seat, I'm afraid the place is a shambles." He made to tidy up the old couch, but mother laid a hand on his arm." Jack, I'm not the Queen of Sheba and besides I'm not sitting down yet. Is your mother asleep?" "No, she will be glad to see you. She was a bit neglected today as I had to get all the potatoes in from the far acre, then my sister Bella couldn't collect Grace, so I had to take her there myself." "It's a terrible thing when the mother goes. I have never seen you looking so lost. Well, I see that the kettle is boiling, so while I am in with your mother, Maggie here will clear up the tea things and wash the dishes. Get your coat off, Maggie." Jack tried to protest. "No, Jack, you do as you are told. Here's the Larne Times[5] never opened and I'm sure you are dying for a read. Sit down man and enjoy it."

He needed no further coaxing and I needed no second bidding, for I felt heart sorry for Jack Kane. I discarded my coat and tam o' shanter and started into the dishes. It looked like a days worth. Jack was engrossed in the paper while I finished, then brushed the floor, rubbed over the big range and refilled the iron kettles. Things were not really dirty, but it needed a woman's touch. Mother seemed pleased with my efforts when she came out. Jack Kane said, "You would hardly know the place now, Aggie. It is nice to be young and have so much energy. You are lucky to have such daughters." "Don't I know it. I think a woman is lost without a daughter or two. I know I will never be forsaken, but Maggie here is not cut out for a worker. When I was her age I could cook and sew and knit socks. Maggie isn't that way inclined." "Well, it would be a queer world if the good God had made us all the same," smiled Jack Kane. "Isn't that right Maggie?" He pulled forward the best chair for mother and seated himself opposite her.

Jack Kane was about forty. He was not bad looking, stockily built with a mop of curly hair and the weatherbeaten skin of a seafaring man. He wore a seaman's jersey and a long pair of rubber boots. "Your mother looks worn out Jack. What she wants at her time of day is rest and quiet. I took a look at wee Jack. He's very pale and his sleep is not natural looking. What did the Doctor say about him?" "Not much Aggie, I'm afraid." He shook his head as if he considered his case hopeless. "Only that we give him a drop of laudanum, he would cry night and day." "Laudanum, but that will retard his growth," gasped my mother. "Sure you know that is a drug, Jack?" Now I looked as if I was engrossed in a magazine, but of course I was listening attentively to all that was being said.

My mother leaned eagerly forward. "Jack, what about me having baby John for a while? In fact, I wouldn't mind having him for good if God in his mercy spares him. I see no sign in the near future of your circumstances changing. That is the reason for my visit tonight." Jack jumped to his feet in sheer astonishment. "You Aggie, Mrs Welsh, my God, have you not enough of your own with a young child yourself, your tea rooms and a bad leg." "Yes Jack and this and that. Sit down, man dear, and listen to me. I am not an invalid and I have two big girls at school who give me a hand. And it would keep them out of mischief. The other day I caught them firing stones and sods at Johnny Hill."

Hearing this, I lowered my head further behind the magazine. In fact I felt no remorse, for it had been a just revenge. The day before we had been coming home from school when Johnny passed us in his pony and trap and for sheer badness he had stopped ahead to give our chums a lift, actually spreading a rug over their legs to make them comfortable, leaving Mollie and me to walk home alone.

"In the spring my other girl Aggie comes home to help in the tearooms and she is just great with children. I am sure my family and I are more fit than your poor mother in there."

"That may be so, Aggie, but I would be less than a man to pass my troubles and responsibilities onto you and take advantage of your unbelievable kindness." "Then call it a selfish desire of mine, Jack. I love babies, especially boys. When one of mine died at birth it broke my heart." "Indeed I know Aggie, and I know how you idolise Jim and David. Your offer is very tempting." He got up and started to pace up and down the kitchen floor. Rupert scrambled from underneath the table and stood looking at his master as if sensing that he was troubled. Then he came and lay down at my feet with his shaggy head on his paws as if he realised he was powerless to help solve life's problems.

"I do have three sisters Aggie, but they have their own families and problems. Mind you, they are very good. They see to the washing and shopping and take turns with Grace. Bella has her this week, but a sick helpless infant is another thing, especially at night. Who wants the trouble?" "Aye, who indeed Jack. It takes one to have that wee bit of extra love in their heart. I have not many qualifications and I lack sadly in many things but I know that I could give your little one tender care. It is the cold hard winter coming in that you have to think about as well, Jack." "I know and my old mother will also need a lot of care. But look here Aggie, what about your man? We have left Davie out of the reckoning. I cannot see a man anxious for another man's child in his house." Mother laughed, "I am the boss Jack. Sure you might know that, with the colour of my hair. Davie wept sore when your poor wife died and he came home from his work last week all worried about your sick child and how you couldn't join your boat again. So what about it Jack. Do I win my case or no?"

By this time my book was tossed aside and my eyes riveted on mother's face. Never had I seen her look so lovely. Her face was flushed and alive with anticipation, her lovely auburn hair full of light as if reflecting her feelings. Her skirt had slipped up a little and there was her boot, telling its own story. Later in life when a great sorrow crossed our path in connection with this child, that scene came back to me in every detail and I shed bitter tears. It has often haunted me down the years with a mixture of joy and sorrow.

"The child is yours, Agnes Welsh, as long as you want him and if the Lord is pleased to spare him. You are the only woman in Islandmagee who I would give my child to. God bless you!" Jack gripped mother's hand with deep emotion. "Well, that is settled then," mother was brisk and cheerful. "Mind you Jack, I can promise no miracle with an ailing infant. I am only an ordinary woman and I know the magnitude of the task I have undertaken. We have heard the doctor's verdict, but I promise by God's grace to do my best for your wee boy." "Oh and Jack, use a bit of good diplomacy with your mother. You must not let her see you think she is incapable of looking after her grandchildren. I spoke about the matter with her tactfully in there. I said I would love to take wee John for a while to help you both out and she whispered "God bless you" and squeezed my both hands hard." "Mother knows full well you are a fine woman, Aggie. Today my troubles seemed unbearable as I was digging the potatoes. What was the end of it going to be, I thought. I felt that I would never smile at life again. Tonight I can sleep with a lighter heart. And Aggie, I don't want to insult you by mentioning money but if the child survives I will help in keeping him in clothes and food. You have your own family to provide for." "Fair enough, Jack. I am only sorry that we will be depriving Grace of her brother, but she can come to see him anytime."

So we prepared to bear Jack Kane's child away from him. I know he was thinking of his lovely wife Mary, taken in the prime of young womanhood. I found it touched me and I was almost in tears. Mother said little as we hurried home, her carrying the baby wrapped in a warm rug and me following with his little bundle of clothes.

Mollie was waiting anxiously for us at the open door. We came into the lamplight and mother's eyes went straight to father's. "Well, David, say it out what you have to say."

"Knowing you Aggie, I think that would be useless. I will say this one thing, I only hope you realise what you have taken on." "Oh Davie, the motherless baby was in sore need of love and with God's help I hope I can give it." He said nothing more but reached out and taking the baby in his arms seated himself by the fireside and removed the rug. Beattie had come down the stairs sucking her dummy and she knelt excitedly beside father and examined the baby's wee pink toes and touched his dolls face gently with one finger. "Poor wee baby, Beattie, he has got no dummy," said mother as she brought forward the old wooden cradle. My little sister studied him carefully. He was waking up now, stretching and looking as if he would cry. Suddenly she pulled her dummy out of her mouth and thrust it against his. "Here baby, you have dummy". It was a complete and final surrender.

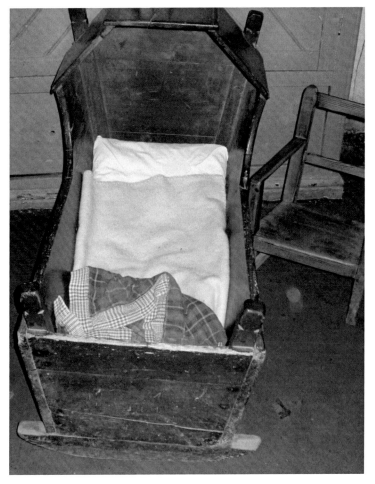

An old wooden cot or crib.

Chapter 5
Trials and Blessings

In Islandmagee Christmas had come and gone, then the New Year ushered in heavy falls of snow and ice with blizzards, our worst for many years. These disappeared as February arrived, but it was a wet mild month bringing much sickness, especially among children and older folk. Now it was the first week in March and it too was living up to its reputation of cold dry days and biting winds. However, there were certainly less germs about and people were beginning to perk up again, despite the cold.

At the Gobbins, our family had had a trying time. Wee John had howled out his distressing cries most days and the nights had been even worse. Dr Dundee[1] said he could do no more and he could not possibly see how the child could survive. Christmas, usually a happy time in our home, was the worst we had experienced. The persistent cries of the baby had wrecked the nerves of all the family. Mollie and I had become more disobedient, for we got tired of hushing John or doing extra chores as mother spent time with him. My brothers were not so keen any more to come home at weekends. Father got irritable and often snapped the nose of mother. The whole pattern of our happy home life seemed to have changed for the worse. There were no more delightful evenings at the fireside reading the Red Letter or the Larne Times.

Now my mother was bad at spelling, her one failing, but she was a gifted reader and could write beautifully. She had a lovely flourish with her pen. When reading to us she could vary her voice and expressions to suit the occasion and pause when necessary. If she had been living in the modern age she could have held her own with any of the television readers. But she had no time to entertain this way now and father felt the loss most.

When Mother talked afterwards about those difficult months, she told us that she had braced herself and tried to keep a calm demeanour. Often she had doubted the wisdom of what she had done and been sorely tempted to take the child back. Why, she asked herself, am I sacrificing my family and husband for this, someone else's duty? She had paced the floor night after night for many long weeks. Lying upstairs, I could sometimes hear her movements, but with the selfishness of youth I was content to seek my comfort in sleep. Of course she wanted me to be rested for school but when I grew older I wished that I had slipped downstairs even if all I could have done was to slip my arms around her to comfort her during her lonely night vigils. My mother said that when she looked into the little face puckered in pain with his fingers clutching her dress as if seeking comfort and relief, she was certain she heard the Saviour whisper, "As long as you have done it unto one of these my little ones, you have done it unto me." She thought too of the lovely fair face of Mary Kane, "I thrust my self pity aside as an evil thing and with His grace I struggled on," she ended.

At long last the tide seemed to turn in my mother's favour. Wee John began to improve, he cried less and now slept until early morning. He had put on a few ounces and in the day time would sleep, or lie contented. Mother had introduced a drop of Daisy's milk into his feed. It was sustaining and had healing qualities suitable for a delicate stomach. It seemed to have worked. Things slowly returned to normal. Mother was now able to resume her reading to father for a few minutes in the evening. The smile was back on his face now and once I heard him say to mother, "You were a wonder to me during those trying months."

It was Saturday a few weeks later. Breakfast was finished and Mollie was rocking wee John off to sleep. I was sitting on a stool blowing on the fire with our new pair of bellows. A pot of potatoes for mother to bake with was bubbling over the heat. The door knocked and Robert Kane, a lad about my own age, came in. "Oh hallo Robert lad. You are nice and early this morning. Take a seat, dear." "My father had to get up early for his boat so I did not lie in. Are Jim and Davie about, Mrs Welsh?" "Aye, they are just over at Woodside's for some bags of chaff. I want to renew the beds because I will soon have the Railway men coming to repair the bridges."

Every year the Railway Company who owned the Gobbins Path and marine walk would send about five or six of their men to mend the bridges, replace those carried away after the winter storms by raging seas or repair the paths. It took a couple of weeks to accomplish their tasks and mother always fixed them up with makeshift beds in the teahouse and made them food. Most of them were married men from the Ballymena area and usually the same ones came every year. My parents loved the 'good crack' and in the evenings some of our neighbours would also call and join in the 'yarning'. Despite our protests, we children were sent up to bed at our usual time and so missed the entertainment.

"How is your mother Robert?" "Great, she says she may have a baby for us soon." "Are you hoping for a sister? "asked Mollie. "I don't mind if it's another brother," Robert said softly. "Meaning you don't like girls," I said, with distain. "If you don't watch what you are doing, you will burn the funnel of those bellows away," retorted Robert. Mother snatched them from me. "That good bellows I paid John Duff[2] seven and six for! Go and wash your face and tidy your hair. You look like a sheep with it hanging in your eyes." Robert turned from the window. "I can see them coming Mrs Welsh, I'll go and meet them." He was away like a hare through the door. "Let him run on," said Mollie scornfully. "He'll be glad enough of us during the week."

Robert was in my class at school. He was a Kane and full cousin to wee

John. He was a nice lad with brown hair and freckled face. The Kane house sat at the top of the Gobbins Brae and at the commencement of Lang Dale. The four Kane boys were our childhood friends, especially Robert and Davie. Robert Kane loved my two big brothers and at the weekends they were inseparable. He also had a high regard for mother and she for him. She never frowned on him no matter how often he turned up at our home and that was most days. Often his own mother would have to come to the stile seeking him. "Robert, Robert," her shrill voice would echo over the hills.

Robert Kane's family lived at the top of Gobbins Brae, where Lang Dale began and runs down to the Middle Road.

My brothers had returned with the chaff and Davie was carrying two big brown paper parcels as well. "Willie Woodside was at the station for the mail train, mother, so he brought our parcels." "They are from Mrs Rankin," Mollie and I shouted in excitement, almost in unison. Soon the tables were littered with the parcel contents and our excitement grew. The boys lost interest when they saw it was 'women's apparel', and headed out. Mother read out Mrs Rankin's letter as Mollie and I tried on the various lovely things.

'My Dear,
I hope you find these things useful. Most of them are used articles with the
exception of the two tweed coats for Maggie and Mollie. I was fortunate
to get them at a sale last week. I have knitted you the shoulder length red
shawl. I don't think it will clash with your hair. With your complexion you
could wear any colour. I know the curtains will be useful, for you could cut
them down for the tearooms at Easter.
No thanks now, dear. It is but a small reward for all your goodness to us
during the summer. Your nice baked bread and the care and cleaning of
the cottage and of course the messages the girls get for us.
I am looking forward to seeing you at Easter, DV.'

"God bless her," said mother. "What a wonderful little woman she is, girls.
I was worrying as to how I was going to get you both clad. Look at these
jumpers and skirts and socks and shirts for the boys too. Now you will both
be able to go to church with your father. God has never failed to provide for
me and my faith has been so small. I don't deserve it."

We had scarcely heard her. Mollie had snapped up a lovely brown frock
from me and I was tugging at her hair as fiercely as I could. "Stop it!" mother
commanded, boxing me on the ear. "You don't deserve anything! Sure you
know that brown would not suit your pale colouring. Let Mollie have it." It
was then that I spotted the pair of lovely black patent court shoes. I snapped
them up and thrust my feet into them. They fitted me beautifully for I had
a high instep and the high heels made me look elegant. "You look like a
duchess in them," smiled mother. I smiled myself. I had never possessed a
pair of shoes before, having only worn a pair of black-buttoned boots or a
pair of heavy boots with protectors.

The boys had returned. "Mother, we are starving. Is there a wee drop of
tea going?" Mother came back down to earth, but she still stood a moment
with the curtains in her hands, imagining how nice they would look at Easter.
"Oh, I forgot about the spuds, they will be into mush! I tell you what boys,
what about a potato with a bit of Holmes's good country butter and a glass
of buttermilk? It will fill us better than tea. No Robert, don't go. You should
know you're welcome to a potato." We were a happy band as we gathered
round the table. Mother emptied the spuds onto a big tray and set it in the
centre while I fetched the buttermilk and glasses. Then it was everyone for
themselves!

As I finished my meal I thought about the Rankin family. Mr and Mrs
Rankin owned a very successful jewellery business in Royal Avenue. They
were a happy devoted couple. Mr Rankin had been a widower and married
again. His new wife was a dainty little English woman and he seemed to
idolise her. They had a teenage son and daughter and Jack, the son, spent his

summer holidays in the company of my brothers. The Rankins rented a small cottage from Mariott Holmes, another big farmer whose land lay adjacent to the Woodsides. You could see their big dwelling house and farm from our little end window, looking way over to the main back road. We called the Rankin's cottage the 'Dolls House'. It nestled in the trees close to the roadside near the farm. From early spring the flower boxes on the window sills were ablaze with colour and in summer lovely striped hammocks were fixed onto the trees in the garden. How I often wished that I could relax in such luxury. Inside the cottage was like a palace, furnished in the best possible taste. Mother never needed to coax us to help her clean it.

"Oh mother, look who is coming", cried Jim who had been looking out the end window.

"Oh no," gasped mother. "It's the Reverend Steen[3] and look at the table and the state of the house." Robert and Davie sprung up from the table, upsetting a glass of buttermilk. "Come on quick, before old Steen gets here." Mother was too late to stop their exit but she shouted after them. "Wait until I tell your father, and you Robert too." For the next few minutes pandemonium reigned. Mother ran with the coal bucket and the potato pot. Mollie swept the potato skins and dishes into a bath and hid it under the sink. She washed the slops off the table and put on a fresh cloth. I chased out Belinda and hurriedly swept up the floor. There was just time to slip upstairs and bring down the carpet mat Nellie had bought us at Christmas. I set it in front of the hearth.

Then 'he' had arrived and was tying his pony to the gate post. Mother met him looking calm and collected. She had managed to tie on a white apron. "How are you Agnes, well I hope?" Steen said in his deep voice. "Come on in sir. Right glad I am to see you."

He was so tall he had to lower his head to come in the door of our cottage. "It is a bad day and a bad time to visit any of my flock, but I had business with Mr Browne and so I decided to come over and see you. My visit is long overdue, but as you know, we have had a lot of sickness and I have been kept at it." "You are always welcome, sir. Sit down." She pulled forward a chair but he stood for a few minutes gripping her hand in his. He was a fine big build of a man and presented a striking appearance with his flowing white beard and full head of white hair. He had a good complexion and keen blue eyes. I had heard mother say that he was then in his late sixties. Reverend Steen turned to Mollie and me and patted us both on the head. I looked up into his face in awe. I had always had the impression in my childish mind that our minister bore a close resemblance to what I imaged God would actually look like. He seated himself, stretching out long legs. By then he had occupied the pulpit of First Islandmagee Presbyterian Church for over thirty years. A fearless and outspoken preacher in the pulpit, he would lash out at anything that displeased him. Mother said that his only weak point was his lack of discretion, but on the whole he was admired and respected by his Islandmagee congregation. A sound, orthodox man who preached the Gospel with sincerity, his pet subject was Temperance. At every opportunity he would strongly condemn the evils of strong drink and was a known authority on the subject. Every June, at the annual Presbyterian General Assembly in Belfast, it was the Rev Steen who gave the report on the yearly sale of liquor in Northern Ireland. He could relate bloodcurdling tales of the havoc and disaster that drinking could have on family life. On a Sunday at church we children were mesmerised by him. He would speak for a while in a low hypnotic voice and then suddenly bellow out so loudly that the very stained glass church windows seemed to shiver and shake.

The Rev David Steen (right) served as minister of First Islandmagee Presbyterian Church for 51 years from 1877-1928. Rev John Elliott, who succeeded him in 1929, is pictured left.

His wife, Matilda Steen, was from Denmark and a stout but very ladylike woman. They had a son and several daughters.

The Rev Steen and my mother discussed events around the Gobbins and the rest of Islandmagee. Mollie and I knew to sit as quiet as lambs and even Beattie was on her best behaviour. Steen asked to see wee John and put his hand on his head in blessing.

"I am puzzled about this child, Agnes. Can you say definitely that he is now legally yours?"

"No sir, nothing was arranged definitely. I felt a pity for the man and the helpless infant."

Steen shook his head. "I think Agnes, that you should look into the matter to safeguard yourself against future sorrow. Of course, Jack Kane may marry again and may not want the child back. And they tell me he is fond of the bottle..." Mother only smiled. "I think he likes a wee drop now and again. Oh Maggie, show Mr Steen the composition you did at school the other day. She got full marks for it, sir." I fetched my schoolbag and handed him my composition. I had entitled it 'The Dangers of Alcohol'.

'Have you ever seen the works of a motor car? No doubt the engine is wonderful but we have in our bodies a more wonderful engine called the heart...' My composition went on to describe the functions of the heart and the disaster which ensued when alcohol was continually taken. "We had a lecture in school the other day, Sir, and it was the subject for our home exercise." I could sense Mollie tittering at me under her breath. "A fine piece of work, Maggie," replied Rev Steen. "It is very gratifying to know that this lecture is being given in schools."

"The kettle is boiling Mr Steen. You will be ready for a cup of tea after your drive." "No, no Agnes. Thank you all the same. I had to partake of dinner at Thomas Brownes[4]. Now, what part of God's word would you like me to read to you and the girls?" " 'The Twenty Third Psalm'[5], Sir, because I had a strange dream a few nights ago where I was in a desert with nothing but sand and more sand and a hot burning sun. It beat down relentlessly and I could not find any way to escape. But suddenly the scene changed and I found myself in soft green pastures where a brook trickled over moss and stones so tranquil and refreshing. I was almost disappointed to wake up and ever since my thoughts have returned to the Shepherd's Psalm." "Beautiful, Agnes. Let us read it then."

His deep, powerful voice seemed to echo over the hills and cliffs, bringing new meaning and life to the old Psalm. Rev Steen himself made an impressive picture as he read, reminding me of one of the Old Testament prophets, like Moses. "As we read it Agnes, you will notice that we walk only in 'Green Pastures', if we yield our lives completely to Him. The 'quiet waters' is that perfect peace which is the portion and possession only of those who know Him as Saviour and Lord. And you young girls," he turned his eyes earnestly upon us. "I would implore you to determine to direct your young footsteps in these 'Green Pastures'. This is the secret of successful living. Oh, that every young life could grasp the great truth - that it is only when we glorify God that we can enjoy Him forever. It is only the Christian who can fully appreciate the temporal blessings of life because his heart is tuned to the Giver of all."

Woodside's farm, Burnside Cottages and Welsh's cottages in 2014.

After these words of counsel, we knelt to pray, with a special blessing for the motherless babe who had come to live in our midst. Rev Steen asked that God's hand of healing might continue upon him. Then mother accompanied him to the door and waited until he disappeared along the path. She came in again brightly, pausing for a moment before she set the griddle on.

"His visits are few girls, for he has a big congregation, but when he does come he brings the benediction of God with its blessings and peace."

Chapter 6
The Belfast Naturalists Field Club

It was wintertime at the Gobbins. The scene was truly magnificent. Although the wind was lessening its intensity, the fury of the waves had not abated. Great breakers came rolling in with renewed vigour, casting spray over the stones and high rocks and seemed to be attempting to reach the path, almost within their grasp. Even Wise's Eye had become a victim to the onslaught. The sea came lashing through the tunnel, barring anyone's approach. Seagulls sheltered in the bosom of the mighty Gobbins cliffs, with only a few daring ones attempting to skim over the raging waves. The waterfall near the entrance to the cliff walk played its part in adding to the turbulent scene. Descending in a roaring torrent over the boulders and mossy stones, it had washed part of the path away, before hastening to become absorbed into the great breakers below.

Away to the right, Blackhead Lighthouse[1] made a dramatic picture, as strong and even more formidable than the angry seas that beat against its walls. In a few hours darkness would descend and the flashing rays of its light would add more fascination to nature's scene.

As I made my way home I glanced over to Hills' house. Their tearoom was still boarded up for the winter. I spotted Annie carrying some driftwood from the shore and when she saw me she waved. She was a nice girl and despite the Hills' quarrel with my family, she had remained friendly with us children. Youth called to youth and in Islandmagee life could be dull enough, particularly in winter, without depriving herself of our company.

Around the bend of the distant low shore I could make out several figures approaching, bent over against the wind. It might be my brothers and Robert Kane returning from their customary Sabbath walk. I turned up my nose as I proceeded up the field with the wind so strong that I had real difficulty keeping my hat on. Sneaks, yes they were sneaks, for Mollie and I were forbidden to accompany them. Several times we had tried, only to be met with sods and stones aimed at us. We had whinged to mother but she had taken their part. Boys would not want girls following them, she said.

Mollie had come back from Sunday school and I had slipped down the field to watch the great winter waves rolling in. I was sent immediately to the well for a bucket of water. Mollie joined me and we fooled about for a bit. We tried to spin round in a circle with the bucket of water without spilling a drop. Mother appeared at the end of the house and called us to hurry. She looked exasperated as she came out of the tea house carrying a number of things. "The next time I send you for water Maggie, go alone. Come on quick! I need you to go to the shop. Four members of the Naturalists Field

Club[2] from Belfast have arrived and they have gone walking by the shore. Mr Davidson said they would be back for tea about six o'clock. I haven't a thing in the house." I realised that was who I had spotted on the low shore. "The shop," I gasped in dismay. "I am going to no shop on a Sunday, mother." "Another word from you Maggie and I will cuff your ear. I cannot tell them that I can make no tea. They are such old friends and I have never been asked to entertain them on the Sabbath before, but I'm sure the good Lord realises this is an exception. I have nothing but a few eggs in the house, so you must go to Strahan's for ham and tomatoes."

I cried bitterly. To have to go and ask Martha Strahan to open their shop on a Sunday felt like asking me to commit suicide. Not only would the Kanes and Johnstons see me going, Martha Strahan herself would be highly indignant if asked to get her keys and go across the field specially to open the shop. But I had been given no choice but to obey, so with the tears blinding me, I hurried away over the hill to the top road, thinking horrible thoughts about how unfair it was that Mollie always got the easy end of it.

By half past five you would not have believed the transformation of our tea room! It looked so cosy and inviting on this winter day. A tremendous fire of whin runts and coals burned in the big wide fireplace. The chairs were drawn near the fire and the table close by was set out with our best dishes, plates stacked with sodas, wheaten bread and lovely printed country butter. A big table lamp on the small table in the corner cast a warm, pleasant glow over the room.

Looking through the Girder Bridge, Gobbins Path.

The Girder or Tubular Bridge on the Gobbins Cliff Path.

The Field Club gentlemen returned punctually, tired and weatherbeaten with healthy appetites. They looked around with keen appreciation. I slipped away shyly to the kitchen, for Mr Blackburn was present and he was the one I was hoping to give my poems to, if I could pluck up the courage. I hoped that confidence would find me as the night wore on.

Mother, an accomplished cook, got the fry going. She fried the slices of ham in a big round pan over the open fire. She cracked in two eggs each, expertly avoiding cracking the yolks. She then fried the tomatoes and several farls of potato bread. It looked so appetising on the dinner plates, ham and eggs trimmed with tomatoes and the potato bread peeping out fanwise from underneath. Each plate was wiped round the edges with a clean linen cloth before it was placed on the tray. Mother was insistent about this.

I could hear a cheer go up outside as Mollie carried in the tray followed by mother with her big blue enamelled tea pot. "I have a message for you, Maggie," mother said later, as I helped her to wash up. "Mr Blackburn wants to see you. Ha! You don't look so sulky now."

I could feel my face light up with pleasure at this news. Father was sitting keeping an eye on wee John as he lay contented in his cradle. He smiled at me. "You have shed enough tears for one day, Maggie. Run on in." But I had something to do first. I quickly ran upstairs and putting my hand under the loose paper near to the thatch, I pulled out my precious hidden poems. I walked shyly back into the tearooms. (Afterwards mother said I did not present a very nice appearance, for I had on a most unbecoming drab frock and as usual my hair needed a good comb and its ribbon tied properly.)

The rest of the Naturalists were asleep or dozing by the fire and I didn't

A crowd of holiday visitors returning from the Gobbins shore.

think they even noticed me. Mr Blackburn bade me sit beside him. I found him a pleasant, goodlooking man. Mother had told me he had several volumes of poems published. "I have brought my poems for you to read," I said timidly. I sat with bowed head and pounding heart as he proceeded to read them. "It is very difficult to say which one I prefer Maggie. Perhaps I would say 'The Snowdrop', because of its spiritual implications. Do we not feel pleased and experience a thrill when we can express our thoughts in verse? The delightful things of life can offer us much blessing and pleasure. God's world is so beautiful and an appreciative eye is a gift God has given to poets like us." "Poets like us." He had classed me as himself. Proud as a peacock, I went back to join my family.

At nine o'clock the party had to be reminded that they had a train to catch at Ballycarry. As usual an envelope was left on the table by the club in thanks for the hospitality given. It contained paper money, no mean gift in those days.

The Snowdrop

Fair lovely lady we welcome thee,
Thy beauty is supreme.
In a dainty bonnet of white
and a slender frock of green.
Thou comest in the winter,
When derelict is the ground.
And every place thou dwellest
True loveliness is found.

When walking through the woods
I have gazed into your face,
Temptation's powers were lessened
and nobler thoughts took place.
I thought of the Holy City,
Of the purity reigning there
Heaven was mirrored in your soul
Oh snowdrop so lovely and fair.

Then I gathered you in my hands,
Making a posy so sweet,
Raising your fragrant loveliness
so close against my cheek.
You then adorned my room,
Chasing the shadows away,
Oh lovely, charming lady,
You have too short a day.

Chapter 7
Easter

In telling the story of my childhood, Easter ranked high in our calendar. The railway workmen came for a few weeks in early April to repair the cliff walk where the iron bridges had become prey to the storms of winter and as soon as they departed, my mother would begin her preparations for the seasons first visitors to Welsh's Tea Rooms. The winter waves had played havoc, leaping up over forbidden territory assisted by the winds, carrying parts of the path away and causing rockfalls. The Northern Counties Railway Company then owned and maintained the Gobbins Marine Walk.

Cliff Path at the Gobbins.

The bridges and wooden walkways at the Gobbins had all to be maintained and repaired each year after the winter storms.

My mother gave their workers accommodation as best she could, using our tearooms as a bedroom, putting some bedding on top of the tables and trying to make them as comfortable as possible. She would send them off with breakfast and then provide a hearty dinner at night. About five or six workers came, fine men from the Ballymena area. In the evenings they would join our parents and some of the neighbours would drop in. The jokes and 'crack', I believe, were great. As I have already said, mother always hounded us up to bed, much to our disappointment and resentment. She also made sure we were not occupying the room off the kitchen during those times.

With the cleaning that followed their departure, there was no chance to dream. It was work and more work. The chimney was first to be cleaned, so mother would climb up onto the porch roof, which had an iron on it, first. Then she would take off her boots and climb in stocking feet, so as not to damage the thatch. With a bag full of straw or old rags she would thrust this up and down inside the chimney. The fire was not lit and another bag had been opened wide and nailed across to catch the falling soot and dust. The tea room had to be cleaned inside and the outside of the house whitewashed with lime. Mother had to do all this, for father was miles away at work, but when he was home he got started into the gardening, preparing to get early potatoes sown. He had one plot near the house and another right beside the Gobbins Cliffs. After stubbing the whins he cleared a big square and dug in good soil where he grew the loveliest floury potatoes. The carrying of manure to feed the plots was the job of Mollie and myself. He wanted to put in his potatoes, so could mother spare us? She did so with good grace, never complaining even though every month wee John was needing and demanding more of her attention. In addition, Tom Browne our landlord, came seeking our help with his farm work. "It is just to scale a few drills of manure, Mrs Welsh," he would say, but this turned out to be two or three days of hard toil. At night we would crawl exhausted into bed to dream of manure and more manure. Browne's farm was the next one past Marriott Holmes's farm on the Back Road. You could see the Holmes' farmhouse and land from our back window. It lay close to Woodsides. Some of the surrounding fields and land, including our cottage, belonged to Tom Browne. Our pay was poor and mother wasn't pleased. "I must put my foot down," she would say. "Just because we live in one of his houses, it seems we must be at his beck and call. God knows we pay our rent regularly." It was also hard work helping father. We carried manure in a bath between us, with a bucket in the other hand down the field over the burn and up another field to the cliff top. Our hands would be blistered from all the carrying. There was some compensation when we stopped to 'take a breather' and cautioned by father to take care, I would go a few steps and peer down over the mighty cliffs to the great depths beneath. I could glimpse the Sandy Cave and the bridge that proceeded on from it. Very soon now, until the late autumn, the visitors would be coming in countless numbers to feast on the beauty of the Gobbins that has never ceased to thrill me.

A few weeks later postman Alfie Jackson had a pile of letters for us. "Tell your mother she needs to employ a secretary," he smiled, as he handed Mollie the mail. We met him at Robert Kane's house, as we came back with 'messages' from Tom Ross's[1], another grocer on what we then called the Upper Road. The letters all contained bookings for the summer, with a few for Easter, which fell in late April this particular year. One was from a very old friend, the Rev Wylie Blue[2], minister of May Street Presbyterian Church in Belfast. As usual, he was bringing his church choir to the Gobbins and mother's catering was always a red letter day for them all. "Girls, I can see a tremendous summer ahead. I may have to send for Agnes earlier on account of having wee John." She frowned as she read out another letter.

Dear Mrs Welsh,
Will you be a dear and do the needful to the cottage. A few of the boys and I spent a quiet weekend there last week and we left a bit of a mess. We had to go back early having engagements in town. Looking forward to seeing you at Easter and anticipating another glorious summer at the Gobbins.
Yours as ever,
Billy Edwards

"That's typical of all men, girls. They seem to think you wave a magic wand and all is done." Fortunately, we had got our holidays from school. Mother went off to sort out the cottage, taking Mollie and Beatrice along with her. I was left to keep an eye on wee John, a task I detested.

Some Queen's University boys from Belfast had been renting the cottage belonging to Woodside's, next door to their own big farm house, for some years now. They included Billy Edwards[3], the well known professional rugby footballer and the Newel brothers. They all came from respectable families and were full of the joy of living. 'A bit of a mess'! Afterwards mother told us the cottage was so bad she had taken Mary Woodside in to see it. The remains of a roast was still there, dried up and smelling. There were plates of stale bread and cakes. Mary looked aghast when she viewed the sink filled with dirty dishes and saucepans, for underneath were lovely cut crystal glasses with a jug to match, but most of them smashed or cracked with the weight upon them. Mother had warned them repeatedly to stack the dishes and keep the glassware separate. "I blame their people," mother had said. "This is the result of having plenty of money. I have a good mind," she added, "to close the door on it all. I have enough on my plate without tackling all this." Mary offered to help but mother wouldn't hear of it. "I'm too much of a grouser, Mary. I forget I have boys of my own. Besides, you have to admit they are all winsome lads."

"Your heart is too big, Mrs Welsh. I consider them young devils, though mind you, they never give us any real bother." Mary said she had never heard a word and she expected they were playing cards and must have left in the early morning. On their arrival one had called for milk and eggs.

Mary Woodside was a handsome, sturdy young woman, fair haired and good natured. Mollie and I often helped her bring the cows in to be milked. She had a favourite brown and white cow called Minnie, with such a large udder that she put all her sister cows to shame. It seemed to me that they followed dolefully behind her, as if only too aware of their shortcomings. There was romance in the air regarding Mary Woodside. She was being paid a lot of attention by a tall thin young fellow named Hamilton Quee[4], who owned his own butchery business on Belfast's Newtownards Road. He visited the farm quite frequently.

I was relieved when mother and Molly returned from tidying the cottage in less than a couple of hours, although wee John had been quite good. He was now sleeping outside in his perambulator. We were just having tea when suddenly shriek after shriek came from the pram. The three of us rushed out, fearful of what to expect. When Mother lifted him he seemed to be wriggling one of his little bare feet. "Look at the marks on his toes, something has bitten him!" The howling continued. Tom Browne's cart horse was grazing close to the fence. "Donald, yes that is it. He must have nipped him." The horse was actually stretching his neck over looking for the titbits he often received. "You old rascal. This is the result of coaxing him up near the house. Shoo him away girls." Poor Donald certainly looked guilty, he trotted away a bit and then stopped and looked back, as if to say, "Would it be any use if a fellow tried to apologise?" John's crying had by now stopped and he was actually smiling.

Easter arrived with good weather, cold but dry. There was an influx of visitors. The curtains from Mrs Rankin and the new wallpaper had transformed our tea rooms into a little palace. We had gathered primroses mixed with modest violets for the tables. Robert Kane had helped us dig out some nice green ferns and the fireplace was arranged with both these and lovely orange blossomed whin bushes, which blended delightfully. The adjoining door between the living room and the tea room was opened up so that Mollie and I could go to take orders and attend to the tables. Our menu was boiled, poached or fried eggs with homemade bread and preserves. Later in the summer it changed to homemade potted meat and our own boiled ham.

The 'Pickie Boys', as the university boys were nicknamed locally, had arrived in full strength for Easter. They had a quick swim at Law's Rock every morning, then romped about the cliffs and caves until the evening, returning to the cottage for a fantastic meal, then a singsong or game of cards. They had been reprimanded about the terrible mess and broken glass of their previous visit. "It will never happen again, sweetheart," said one of the Newel boys, putting his arm around my mother's waist. Little did we realise that he was right, that soon the day would come when we would never see that fair boyish face again, when the Great World War would claim him and many of his pals.

Mr and Mrs Rankin and family had also arrived for Easter to their 'dolls house'. We had a lovely fire going to welcome them and primroses picked. Mother sent over a selection of her home baked breads: soda, wheaten, potato and oaten.

For Easter, my brothers had erected a new sign along the garden head overlooking the low shore. It looked well, a big board with supporting posts printed in good clear letters.

WELSH'S TEA and REFRESHMENT ROOMS

Picnic Parties Catered For

It was a very happy Easter time for all. It was lovely renewing friendships after the winter months of separation. Wee John made new friends and got lots of attention. He seemed to enjoy the fuss made of him, smiling and gurgling, on his best behaviour. So many visitors wanted to nurse him. On the Easter Tuesday night, when most visitors had gone home, mother, who was absolutely exhausted, was enjoying a rest at the fireside. Father was out and about in his gardens. The boys were away to Mullaghboy Corners for a bit of fun. Mollie had gone over to the Burnside to play with some Belfast children. This seemed a good chance for me to try and finish my poem. It had been hard going over the Easter weekend and I was tired too. It seemed as if mother understood my longing, for she smiled as I searched for my pen. "Away into the tearoom, Maggie, no one will disturb you there. God knows when you will get a chance again." I laughed, "A poet must be in the mood, mother. You cannot take up your pen any minute of the day." "You are always in the mood, dear. I heard you talk in your sleep the other night and it was all about bees and skies and lapping waves... Who on earth do you take after? None of my family were that way inclined, or your father's either." "You did not dig deep enough into your ancestry, mother," I retorted, as I hurried away into the tearoom. It had been a hive of activity all day long - now it was still and peaceful. For some weeks now, I had been writing a poem in my head. Now I just had to get it written down.

Spring

Spring is here so bright and clear
Happiest season of the year
Hark to the birds at early morn
See the lambs just newly born.

Chapter 8
The Daring Feat

Willie Holmes[1] looked up from his painting when he saw me. "You are ridiculously thin, Maggie Welsh, your legs are like spiders and what is that ridiculous contraption over your shoulders? I can't say that I've noticed it before." "It's terrible, Willie," I said miserably. "Mother made it for me some time ago and I absolutely hate it!" "You are late home from school too. Mollie and the Kanes passed here over half an hour ago." "It was my rotten old drawing that I had to stay and do again. We had to draw a yacht." "I expect yours was more like a butterfly." laughed Willie Holmes. "Never mind, the summer is here and you will soon get your holidays." "Yes, and I believe it is going to be a smashing summer. Lots of new visitors are coming to the Gobbins. Mother has had a letter from John Elder, the leader of a mission hall from Templemore Avenue and she is going to give his party board and lodgings for the Twelfth week in July. "Say no more girl, I don't want the holidays spoiled with those prudes." "But Willie, I believe the party of about eleven young men and women are all good Christians and I heard mother say one of them in particular, Harry Benson, is a saint of God, so maybe you will change your mind." But he merely smiled with distain and went on painting the windowsill. Willie Holmes was a near neighbour. He lived with his aunt in one of the row of cottages known as the 'Coastguard Cottages'. He was a Holmes of the Gobbins, the 'gentry' of Islandmagee. His family owned 'Gobbins House', the farm I previously mentioned which you could see from our cottage. A family dispute had resulted in Willie leaving home, bag and baggage, and going to reside with his aunt, Miss Wilson[2], in the Lang Dale. Willie was an interesting character, a likeable fellow but with a mind and will of his own. He had been an 'ocean going' sailor for some years but had retired young and was enjoying his retirement and wealth immensely. He was lithe of figure and sported a little moustache. Sometimes he would fix you with a penetrating glance with his fine grey eyes. Willie had no apparent vices for he did not smoke, drink or go to dances. However, he claimed to be an atheist and never attended church, mocking religion or any professing Christian. Despite this, he was well liked around Islandmagee. "He's just wild of heart," my mother would affirm. "Some day a good woman will be the making of him." Sure enough, her prophecy came to pass later on in life.

Willie visited our home frequently and had always something to report. He loved a bit of fun and always got the local lads into mischief. If he was not at some corner with them devising some prank, he would be in someone's house telling amazing yarns about his life at sea when his ship docked for a time in foreign ports. If a concert was held, Willie Holmes would be in the back seats with the lads and he would cause an uproar to such an extent that on one occasion he was asked to leave. Once he tied the handle of old Sam Duff's door to a post outside and poor Sam was a prisoner in his own hut for almost half a day. On another occasion he put a row of clothes pegs around the back of a lady's fur coat as she stood up to sing the National Anthem. The poor woman walked about elegantly, unaware of how she was now dressed.

My parents told us a remarkable story of Willie's daring feat. It happened before I was born, around 1902 I think. It was more than a nine day wonder and for a long time afterwards Willie's achievement was the talk of Islandmagee. He had defied all attempts of friends and neighbours to put him off because it was considered far too dangerous. Undaunted, Willie set his plan into action. Four or five local men volunteered to hammer iron stakes into the rock formation and soil close to our garden at the Gobbins Head. Willie was strapped into an old armchair secured with chains and ropes affixed to the stakes and armed with a small hard brush, (to clean the rock surface before he painted), a tin of white paint and a paintbrush, he was lowered slowly down over the first great cliff face. Those holding the ropes manoeuvred them into position on his commands. I believe quite a crowd came to watch with bated breath. Eventually the bold clear white letters of 'Welsh's Tea Rooms' appeared across the cliffs and Willie was hauled up triumphantly to safety.

Father and mother did not appreciate Willie's impromptu advertising of their business. No one had asked for their approval and he had not told them what he was attempting. Mother said her first thought was of the Hills and what they would think. It would be the first thing to greet them every morning, for the cliff was easily visible from their cottage. She feared they would think it had been deliberately planned to publicise their business. She had covered her eyes and vowed that something would have to be done to that Willie Holmes. However Willie, his confederates, and indeed all those involved, considered it to be a tremendous achievement and so it was. It had taken tremendous courage with the seas sweeping in underneath him and looking up occasionally at the great height above him as he moved cautiously bit by bit along the cliffs painting with letters perfectly spaced. He told me that at times he felt he was falling down into a great abyss.

News of Willie's daring escapade got around and there was an increase of visitors and the tearooms trade. Mother told us cameras flicked and reflicked and in England and Scotland and indeed further afield, Willie made headline news and was considered a great hero. I believe old Sam Duff had stood laughing and wheezing and called it not only a great joke, but also a masterpiece. An Islandmagee captain, asked by our parents what it looked like from the bridge of his ship, had answered. "When you come up Belfast

The Gobbins, Islandmagee.

Some lettering is just visible on top of cliff head, possibly the remains of Willie Holmes's daring painting escapade.

Lough, past Blackhead Lighthouse and then into view of the Gobbins, it seems as if Almighty God has reached down and printed the words there with a bold hand."

The June roses climbing up by the windows of Willie's home made a nice splash of colour against the whitewashed walls. It was a glorious day, and I was glad of the break to chat to him. The strap of my hideous school bag was cutting into my shoulders through my thin summer frock. "Who are you talking to, Willie?" His aunt, Miss Wilson, came out to the door. "Oh, it is you child. I was wanting to see you. Come on in, I have some more books for you." I needed no second bidding, although I was in awe of Miss Wilson. She was an elderly woman with a very masculine appearance. She was tall and wellbuilt and had a deep mannish voice. Her iron-grey hair was pulled back severely from her face and rolled in a coil. She had the same keen eyes as her nephew. I had one thing in common with her and that was books. It was sheer pleasure to go into her home for everything indicated that she was a reader and books dominated the living room. Magazines were on the table and around the walls were shelves full of books. A magnificent glass bookcase contained volumes of Dickens which gazed out upon me in splendour. An educated woman, Miss Wilson read books far beyond the range of the average reader, but she also had a good supply of fiction. "I have a couple of Annie S. Swann[3] for your mother to read to your father and here is one for yourself. I have finished reading it, so you can keep it."

"'Beulah'," I gasped in amazement, "'Beulah', by Evans Wilson[4]. Oh, I have always wanted to read this, Miss Wilson." She laughed at my enthusiasm. "Well child, you have had your wish fulfilled. And I think I might have a few more of that type."

For once I was glad of my canvas schoolbag, packed full when I left her house. I hurried past the Kane's house, glad none of them were about. They were probably enjoying the sun in their back garden. My bag weighed heavily as I came down towards the stile over the brow of the hill and I gladly took a rest.

Willie Holmes's once famous painting on the cliff face was barely discernible now. Time had accomplished it's work, along with the wind and rain, so that now only the shape of an 'S', or part of a 'T' remained. Today the Lough was glorious, so placid, with scarcely a ripple. The cliffs were basking in the sunshine and the cows grazing in the meadow. They seemed contented, save for the occasional swishing of their tails to stop the flies and pests peculiar to cattle annoying them. Some of the Burnside visitors were having a picnic out in the meadow before the cottages. I was aghast when I noticed so many visitors at the shore, apart from some swimmers who were swimming from Law's Rock to rocks further out to sea. Quite a crowd of visitors were walking up the short slope to Hill's Tea House. Annie was dressed in her white apron, serving tea at the tables outside. Another large party had passed Hills and were climbing the path up to our home. Mother would be furious with me being late home from school.

I hurried quickly over the stile, the weight of my schoolbag forgotten. Perhaps I could make a detour round the back and slip in unnoticed. For not only was I late, but my frock was far from clean and my curly fair hair, my one redeeming feature, had lost its ribbon at some point during the school day. Fortunately mother and Agnes were already so busy serving tables, that I could slip in quietly. Only Mollie looked sourly at me while continuing her work. I lost no time in tackling a stack of dirty dishes as if my life depended upon it. For the next couple of hours or so the pace never slackened. Mother passed me a few times, but she made no remark. Hopefully she could see I was making up for lost time. It was unbearably hot and I wiped the sweat from my face, but everyone else was similarly affected. There seemed no end to the piles of dishes. At least the tourists were enjoying their tea. I could hear their laughter and the blends of Scotch and English accents.

I heaved a sigh of relief when, eventually, the last of the visitors departed. Mother suggested, to our delight, that we could have a good meal ourselves

The Gobbins, Islandmagee

Gentlemen and one well dressed lady on the rocky Gobbins shore.
Note the lady has come prepared with hat and umbrella.

before tackling the remainder of the dishes. One visitor had left half a
dozen bananas and the tourist party guide had brought mother a box of
pastries. One of these was left for the sweettoothed Daisy, although secretly
I thought it was wasted on her. We had a delightful meal under the shade of
the hawthorn tree. During the fuss of the afternoon, mother had put John
and Beattie in the field with their toys and she said they had been extremely
good. Then, while mother went to prepare our father's meal, the rest of us
finished clearing up the tearoom. Agnes carried countless buckets of water
from the well and filled up the empty rainbarrel, all ready for the next day of
dishwashing. With some effort, I was able to snatch an hour before dark to
escape to my favourite tree with 'Beulah'.

Chapter 9
The Pigs

Hughie Wilson[1] scratched his head thoughtfully. "I doubt the wisdom of your mother in sending you girls for the pigs. Couldn't your brothers have come for them?" "That is what I told mother," Aggie replied, "but she turned a deaf ear. I felt like telling her to wrap the boys in cotton wool." "You are the one called Aggie. Are you home for the summer now?" "Yes," Aggie replied sharply. Islandmagee farmers could all be a bit inquisitive. "I bet you were courtin' in the big wicked city. You're a fine lookin' girl." "Mr Wilson, we had better get these pigs home or mother will give us a lecture." "Very good, but mind you'll have to be careful. It would never do if you injured them in any way. It would be a big loss to your mother. Come into the pig house and we'll put them into the sacks."

We followed him into where three wee piglets were awaiting us. At first it seemed great fun, a novelty, carrying a live pig over our backs. We sang as we walked along the lane.

"A pig in a poke, oh what a joke." Soon however, the pigs seemed to weigh more heavily and become harder to hold. "It won't be long until we are home, girls," Aggie called out cheerfully, as she led the way. "As long as we don't meet any of the boys at the foot of the Gobbins Brae." "What a hope, laughed Mollie. "Sure it's after seven o'clock. They'll be there already." We reached the stile leading into William McKeen's[2] fields and were about to go over the field to the back road which would bring us out nearly opposite Marriott Holmes's when for some reason one pig began to squeal, setting the others off. Possibly we were jostling them too much. Their cries attracted a herd of grazing bullocks who decided to investigate and came trotting towards us. "Run for your life," yelled Aggie, "get through the hedge anywhere!"

We ran bravely on, holding our burdens. The fence loomed near but so were the advancing bullocks who had quickened their pace. We could almost feel their hot breath on the backs of our necks. The pigs were by now making a terrible din. With a supreme effort, Aggie hurled herself through the prickly hedge, dragging us after her. The pigs in their sacks fell roughly onto the roadside but we did not care. Aggie was badly shaken and an ugly scratch on her face began to bleed. Mollie and I burst into tears. "I don't care about the old pigs," I sobbed, pulling at my shredded stockings. "Neither do I," said Mollie, examining the ripped sleeve of her dress. By now the bullocks had ground to a halt and stood eyeing us balefully over the hedge. Aggie just wanted to get us all back home, but her problems were not over. As she went to raise her sack to her shoulder, a hole had appeared through which a curly pig tail protruded. "I will just have to manage," she wailed, but as we moved off and turned the bend in the road we found the local boys already gathered. Aggie herself was now on the verge of tears. "Don't stop whatever you do girls, hurry on past." Nothing so dreadful had ever happened to her before. It was terrible to be caught in such an undignified position. The pigs seemed to have survived but they were squealing again, only adding more embarrassment to our situation. As we approached the boys they were sizing up our situation, seeing the sorry state we were in with Aggie desperately trying to keep her pig in its bag. Bob Heddles[3] came forward and relieved Aggie of her sack. He tied a secure knot in the bottom and catching it at both ends slung it over his shoulders with ease. "Don't worry," he smiled at her. "It's not as bad as a bad marriage." "Oh Bob, I never want to see a pig again for the rest of my life!" The rest of the boys followed Bob's example and came to the aid of Mollie and I.

Herby Lynas and Sam Hawthorne took a pig each. They began to imitate the pigs with squeals and grunts. Both boys walked on either side of Mollie and left me more or less to my own company. I had never been popular with the boys. They would tolerate my company only when they could do no better, but if any of my sisters were around, I was ignored. I suppose this gave me an inferiority complex, although I did not know what it meant then, only that I suffered agonies unknown to anyone else when I was growing up.

I hurried on to tell mother, who was anxiously waiting at the door, what had befallen us. Between the tears she heard it all. "The good pigs. Surely you did not injure them," she cried. The boys assured her they appeared none the worse. Freed from their sacks in the pig house the wee beggars ran to poke their snouts through the clean straw. "Girls, look at the state of you! I am truly sorry, now I realise I should have sent your brothers. But they say that a wee cup of tea covers a multitude of sins. So come in all of you. I have a big plate of pancakes on the hob."

Young healthy appetites need no second bidding. Aggie hurried to improve her appearance and Mollie and I soon followed her. "Goodness, when your father sees those scratches I will be in for it girls. He will say I lacked foresight in sending you for the pigs." But already we were feeling better and Aggie and Bob Heddles were too engrossed in each others company to notice that the pancakes were rapidly disappearing. Herby Lynas had started on his fifth!

"Who would like to go to a grand concert tonight in Kilcoan School?" Mother held up pink tickets. "Oh mother, you precious, precious darling." The three of us hugged her close. We had begged her all week to let us go. Her reply had ever been, "And where do you think I would get three shillings for tickets?" "Harry Long[4] is going to recite 'The Bootblack White'," I said excitedly. "Yes, and possibly, 'How Did the Lassie break the Boul?'. That's his best one," said Mollie. "And there's going to be a three act play," added Sammy Hawthorne, helping himself to another pancake, "about divorce over the head of a pair of woman's stays." Everyone, including my mother, roared with laughter and the tea bubbled up my nose. Herby Lynas started to dance round with wee John in his arms and Bob edged nearer to Aggie. It was a happy domestic scene. We were fast forgetting about our traumatic journey with the pigs and the day ended on a more cheery note.

Chapter 10
Ships in the Night

July greeted us this particular year with sunny days, blue cloudless skies and tranquil sea. Each morning the sun rose in the heavens as if determined to outshine the day before. "It is nice to be alive on a morning like this," my mother would say. I remembered her expression and repeated it myself down the years when a glorious day dawned. We children had got our holidays and the work was going on with full swing. The great weather brought large crowds to the Gobbins. There had been endless enquiries, with many wanting to come for two meals. This involved replying back and we children had to help with the correspondence as best we could. The Rev Wylie Blue from May Street Presbyterian Church in Belfast had been a visitor to our tearooms for many years. He often brought his church choir on their annual outing. The menu served was chiefly home made boiled ham or potted meat, both my mother's specialities, along with home baked bread and preserves. Fries and poached eggs were also greatly in demand as the fresh Islandmagee air seemed to give every visitor a healthy appetite. In addition to all this catering, the young folk from the Iron Mission Hall in Templemore Avenue, Belfast had arrived to board for the Twelfth week with us. If not for the fact that one of their members, Harry Benson, was a special

HILL'S PORT, THE GOBBINS, NEAR WHITEHEAD.

Fishermen at Hill's Port, on the Gobbins shore.

friend to our family, Mother would not have taken on this extra work. But mother just loved Harry. "Just to look at his face does my heart good," she said. And she would tell him, "I do not know any girl who would be good enough for you," to which Harry smiled and said, "then I will have to remain a bachelor until you get a divorce, Mrs Welsh."

Mother had made a makeshift bed up for us in one of the outhouses where fuel was stored in winter and had prepared the loft to accommodate six young ladies. Some pink linoleum was found to cover the floorboards and we put nice bedlinen on the beds. The five lads were to sleep on camp beds in the tea room and they were determined to get off early each morning, leaving the tea room ready to serve breakfast and for the daily visitors. They all insisted they would take turns washing the dishes. "Anything is a pleasure, Mrs Welsh, as long as we can stay the holiday week with you," their leader John Elder had said. "What holiday?" we thought. But at least they appeared happy to muck in and help. They were a friendly group and on the Sabbath morning invited us to join them in morning worship. Father was asked to choose his favourite hymn. Harry Benson stood between my parents and in a lovely tenor voice joined in singing 'Rock of Ages'. The morning sunlight streamed in through the little windows and fell softly upon their upturned faces. I thought of the 'green pastures' that the Rev Steen had talked about. Surely indeed this morning we were dwelling in such green pastures. My young heart was touched for the first time and I was confronted with eternal issues. There was not a shadow of a doubt about it. It was lovely to see these young people on the threshold of life having Christ as their master. They had surely found the secret of living. One of the young girls led the prayer. She was bubbling over with the joy of the Lord and there was no mistaking her sincerity. I studied Harry Benson. He was truly handsome, tall and dark with lovely eyes and a manly figure. There was just something attractive about him, not merely in his outward appearance but that his soul seemed to be reflected in his face. It glowed with an inward quality of Christian grace and meekness. John Elder, the group's leader, was of smaller build than Harry. He was a bright young man with a fine head of ginger hair, on the best of terms with his party.

The Sunday dinner menu was stewed meat with rich brown gravy, carrots, peas and potatoes, a pudding of cornflour and jelly, followed by tea and biscuits. At around half past eight that evening the group met again in the open air, on the flat rocks just through Wise's Eye. It made a splendid setting on such a glorious July evening, with the rocks jutting out to sea and the sea coming into the bay at the entrance to the marine walk and the majestic cliffs in the background. In the distance, the outline of Bangor and the Down coastline were clearly seen. The sun was still shining in splendour and it seemed as if God smiled upon them also.

The group started with the grand triumphant hymn, 'He threw out the lifeline to me'. A girl with a beautiful voice sang the verse and the others joined in the chorus. By this time a crowd of spectators had begun to gather. The university boys from 'Gobbin Farm', passing on their way to the bridges, decided to stop and listen. My brothers and their chums came and sat on the rocks. Aggie, Mollie and myself sat beside them and I saw some Burnside people there also. I was amazed to see Willie Holmes appear, although he kept his distance. He was looking remarkably well dressed, wearing a nice suit with white shirt and tie. I fancied I spotted a look of amusement in his eyes. Never before had the gospel hymns been echoed or reechoed round the mighty cliffs and sea.

Well dressed visitors cross a steel girder bridge at the Gobbins after the Marine Walk opened in 1902 (from an old glass negative, with kind permission of Henry Burns).

For the next twenty minutes John Elder spoke convincingly on the text, 'The fool has said in his heart there is no God'. "I am often asked," he said, "in these trying times of famine and disaster abroad, and even with the bloodshed and other forms of evil going on here in Ulster, if there really is a God. Why does He not do something about it? "Friends", I have replied, God has done something about it. He sent His only Son, the darling of his bosom, to die for our sins at Calvary. It is not why does God not do something about it, but rather what are we going to do about it? The fool has said in his heart there is no God. Of course he is a fool. Look around you at this scene of nature and then dare to say there is no God." Elder spoke of God's handiwork, the beauty of creation and of the seasons. Then returning to the spiritual realm, he asked them to consider God and how he had given his son to redeem fallen mankind. Of his perfect life here on earth. His well beloved Son becoming sin for us that he might bring us to God. His fine manly voice carried well and the audience seemed captivated by his words. They listened in rapt silence, scarcely averting their eyes from his face. The service ended with the hymn, 'Will your Anchor Hold', and its grand chorus, 'We have an anchor that keeps the soul'.

It was some time before we began to disperse. Edna Whyte, one of the young mission hall girls, was writing something for Aggie in her recently purchased autograph book.

"Surely you do not believe all that rubbish you have been engaged in?" said a voice. Edna turned sharply to find Willie Holmes addressing her. "Of course I do, otherwise I would not be here. Your soul must be very dark indeed, if you consider it rubbish," she replied quite calmly. "I do not see the need for Mission halls anyway. Surely there are plenty of empty churches?" "I agree,"she said. "But sometimes churches are so bound with rules and rituals and regulations that the simpler message of the Mission Hall has its appeal." "I consider the Mission Halls a place for gossip, where girls hope to get a man. I have been told about them." We could see Edna's cheeks flush and there was a strange sparkle in her eyes. She turned to face him resolutely. "I consider you very impertinent, sir, seeking me out, a stranger, and addressing me in such a manner. I would have you know that the Mission Hall exists solely for the proclamation of the gospel. Speaking for myself and my girl friends, the thought of getting a man, as you term it, has never entered our heads. I personally have more important things to think about, for in the first week in August I am sailing to India from Southampton as a missionary!" She turned on her heel and walked away. I am certain Willie had never been spoken to in such a fashion before. I noticed that he stole away by himself, without talking to anyone.

Edna Whyte seemed a pleasant girl in her light summer frock. She had a sweet expression and wore her long fair hair in two large plaits coiled around the back of her head, which gave her a Madonna-like appearance. Now her curiosity seemed to have been aroused by Willie Holmes and she questioned us further about him. Even more surprises were in store during that week. On the following Tuesday evening, when the rest of the group had walked to Whitehead, I looked towards the cliffs and there were Willie and Edna standing together at the fence looking down to the shore below. "Mother, do you see what I see?" I gasped. Tripping over my words in excitement, I shouted for Mollie to come.

Mother laughed as she gave the fire a poke. "Now, you know just as much as I do. When Willie arrived over this evening, I mentioned that all the young folk were away out except Miss Whyte as she had writing to do in connection with her work abroad. Quick as lightening he went into the tea room and shortly after I saw them walk out." Mollie and I were excited. "Oh mother, it is simply lovely. Do you see that they are attracted to each other. Edna will now cancel all her arrangements." "Auch Maggie, your romantic notions are running away with you. I cannot conceive of a girl of Edna Whyte's type sacrificing her principles so easily. But maybe he has stirred her heartstrings a bit, which speaks a lot for Willie." But alas, it seemed that my hopes of romance were not to be fulfilled. Mother was very decent and told us a little of what had been confided to her. In Edna's attempt to convert Willie, her own personal feelings were involved, but she sternly and resolutely set them aside and accepted it as a test before she would go forth in the Master's name. "I think God sent him across my path, Mrs Welsh," she said, "that I might turn him round about and send him in the right direction."

The remainder of the week found Willie often in their company. If he was late in appearing they would not go on without him and he was to be seen walking with Harry Benson. The weather was still glorious and the young people determined to enjoy it to the full. One of the boys, in a jolly mood, asked mother did she know of a good trick they could play on the girls. Mother had no hesitation in replying, "Willie Holmes is your man for that, son, I know it to my cost." It seems that Willie was consulted and was willing to oblige. That night it was near midnight when the group had said their goodnights and as usual the girls proceeded to their loft bedroom. Suddenly from above came wild shrieks and pandemonium reigned as they fell over each other down the stepladder screaming. "Oh, Mr and Mrs Welsh, there are hideous creatures in our beds." The boys had appeared at the scene looking innocent. When some of the young ladies realised they were clad only in their night attire, they made to rush upstairs again. Perhaps it was better to face the creatures than to be found in this embarrassing predicament. Mother, realising their plight, brandished a brush and ordered the boys to make themselves scarce. Then she went up to the loft to see what awful monsters were lurking there. Under the bedcovers were seven or eight big crabs crawling about. She fetched a pair of gloves and removed the offending creatures. The largest was probably handpicked by Willie. "God bless me girls, but the fellow goes too far. What is to be done with him?" When calm was eventually restored, the girls were able to laugh about it, but they still vowed to get their own back before the end of the week.

Alas, that happy time flew by on wings and keen disappointment was expressed that the innocent time of fellowship and fun was at an end. New friendships had been made and on the Saturday morning departure Harry Benson made a prayer of thanksgiving for their great time together. He asked for a special blessing on my parents and that God's love would protect and enfold the little boy who had come into our home to give us so much joy. Willie Holmes was mentioned with affection. Harry thanked God that the group had been privileged to meet him. He believed that by their Christian witness, Willie's complete outlook on life had been changed. Life was short and it was possible that some of them might never meet again, but he hoped that by God's grace they would all meet around the Saviour's feet and that the circle would be unbroken. I glanced at Edna Whyte and saw the tears run unchecked down her cheeks. Surely her thoughts would be turning to her new life in a faraway land, but perhaps the memory of the Gobbins would remain with her. Even my mother was wiping at her eyes with the corner of her apron.

Our farewells could not be prolonged further, as our next summer guests were soon to arrive. The Rev Wylie Blue and his choir were coming and I had to hurry off to Mrs Browne's for eggs and a can of sweet milk. Such was life's busy day.

Chapter 11
Unique Characters

Reader, I have already introduced you to one of the unique characters of my childhood and it gives me great pleasure to introduce some more. I thank God that I was so privileged to meet them once and the thoughts of them still delight me now that I am grown old myself. I have not forgotten my mother's words regarding old Sam Duff. Yes, in today's modern world such characters are almost extinct and we are so much the poorer. They did add so much interest and colour to life.

Jeammie Morrow, the 'pot scrubber man', was also a familiar figure round our district. He gathered heather from the local hills which he made into scrubbers, whisks and besoms or brooms. He walked round the doors selling his wares. Jeammie had an appreciative eye for beauty and for a considerable time he took up residence near the Gobbins, living in a cave along the shore with his brother Andy. One day I recall he was about with his wares and he summoned up the courage to tell my mother that his scrubbers were increasing from two pence to three. "What is the meaning of this, Jeammie?" mother demanded. He stood before her, a small but alert figure and in his characteristic manner replied with all seriousness and solemnity, "Ah Mam, don't you know the price of heather has increased considerably." With the new price increase accepted and with his bag over his shoulder, he was away over the whin hill again with purposeful step, happier than a king on his throne.

Scrubber Jamie

'I'm Heather Jamie the scrubber man, A wanderer from birth
I never had a hunch for work, Since I struck this blinking earth
My feyther's name was Andy Bann, They called my mother 'Phemie'
As I trog about the weans all shout, "Ma, here's oul' scrubber Jamie."
(First verse of a poem by Charlie McIlroy)

Another character of interest was Robert Grant the thatcher who visited Islandmagee. Of course when I was young, there were many thatched dwellings and plenty of work for the thatcher. 'Rabbie', as he was affectionately known, preferred to eat his lunch out in the open. When he came to thatch, he always brought his own food, tea being his only requirement. We children loved it when Rabbie would come to thatch our home, sometimes only a repair or after long intervals to strip it and renew the old thatch. He would spread out a big red and white spotted handkerchief on his knee. Rabbie was very partial to current bread with jam on it. Immediately the sparrows would come chirping around him hopping over his feet looking for share, perhaps also realising that he was going to make their home in the eaves more comfortable and secure. Rabbie was a tidy little man and a skilled craftsman.

James Moore the pig killer was not quite so welcome a visitor, at least to us children. We would run and hide until the terrible murderous ordeal was over. The big iron kettles would be put on the hob and open fire to boil. James, another small but sturdy middle-aged man, would put on his yellow oilskins and approach his victims armed with rope, ratchet and knife. When we emerged again the pigs would be hanging up in the outhouse with their bellies sliced open, the insides removed and pieces of sticks placed inside to keep the carcasses open. Boiling water was used to scrape and wash their hides. On the table inside would be sitting a big dish of pigs liver and my brothers would be keen to make excellent footballs out of the blown up bladders. After his work was finished, James Moore would wash his oilskins and fold them away neatly, before sitting down for a well-earned meal.

As a child I was fascinated by the tramps that occasionally passed through Islandmagee and never feared them. I actually envied them their outdoor life and their disregard for the normal conventions. My sister Beattie, just recently started school, had a horror of them. "I cannot go to school tomorrow," she would say. "Stephen Greer has been on the Upper Road every day." "Just because he is a tramp, does not mean he is bent on chasing you," I would retort. The beauty and allure of the countryside is worth many a sacrifice and I am certain that it was not always poverty which made them take to the roads. One day when I began to write about them, I had the amusing thought that just as Beattie dreaded tramps, I had the same feeling for goats, at least our one! I was determined I would never write a poem about Daisy. Beattie however, loved Daisy like a mother, and when she put her arms around her, Daisy made no objection. Beattie said she intended to have a herd of goats when she grew up. In later years that prophecy came true, although she only had one goat.

Sadly, today such interesting and colourful characters are now almost a thing of the past.

Chapter 12
Gathering Shadows

'Hi, ho, old heely hod, away we go and fire the sod'. Sod after sod was rained down on Johnny Hill, missing him by a narrow margin. We laughed delightedly and put more effort into it. We had caught him in the act of trying to cut away the steps we had made from the path below up to our garden shed.

Mother had told us there had been a law suite at one time. The Hills had claimed that this particular bit of land, known as the garden head, was their property. Tom Browne had also laid claim to it. The result had made it Browne's legal property but we had permission to use it for our goat to range and to erect our big signboard which read 'Welsh's Tea Rooms'. It sat in a splendid position on the heights overlooking the shore. Today we were hiding behind this sign to fire down the sods.

When the Railway company had taken control of the famous Gobbins Path Walk, Johnny Hill had got a nice little job with them - keeping the paths tidy and and reporting any storm damage, but Johnny was over zealous and at every opportunity he would try to take a good slice with his spade out of Tom Browne's land. Father had cut steps out on the other side of the path also, so that we could walk along a bit and then look down unto the shore below. Johnny had also attacked this with his spade. It became the usual pattern to come out and find no steps. Father would not allow my mother to interfere, saying that Tom Browne had enough to do without worrying him about it. The ground was useless for anything but grazing a goat. But today we had caught Johnny in the act, and aided by Robert and David Kane, we decided to teach him a lesson.

"Hi, we'd better stop" Robert cried, "that sod hit him." Oh gosh, he's coming after us." Johnny Hill was yelling as he climbed up towards us. We made a hurried retreat, making it appear as if we were going away into the far corner of the height to hide, but actually crouching down as we jumped the hedge. We made quickly for home, going in the back entrance. We were breathless and mother looked up alarmed. "It's nothing," I said, "we were just trying to see who could get here first." Unsuspecting, mother returned to cutting Wee John's hair. She beamed affectionately at him in his high chair. "That is the good boy to sit so still." John was now a sturdy lad of over two years. Although small for his age, he was wiry and good natured. "I will be able to get Donald soon and go for a bag of flour for you, Mammie," he said in his little manly voice. "Yes soon darling, you are nearly a big man now and Tom Browne will lend you Donald," replied my mother tenderly.

I had recovered my breath by now and looking at mother's face I forgot all about Johnny Hill. I knew that she thought of wee John as her own, she even talked about what she would send him to do when he grew up. Not to sea, she said. She honestly thought that Jack Kane had given up any notion of wanting him back. He was mostly away at sea anyway and we hardly saw him these days. Every evening John would wait for father to get a ride on his bicycle and my brothers could not get home quick enough at weekends to see him. Beattie and he were no angels, they had the odd fight, but on the whole were good pals.

David slipped out to spy the land and came back to whisper that Johnny was cutting grass at the side of his house, so we had escaped this time. Robert and David set off home but hastily returned to tell us that Daisy was caught on wire at the far corner of the field. Her piteous cries had alerted them. "She looks bad, Mrs Welsh, she's covered in blood." "Oh no," mother cried in distress. "Run Mollie quick to John Woodside's and ask him to send someone for the vet." "Maggie, you mind the youngsters."

Aggie had arrived in, and catching a rug, scissors and some clean linen she ran with mother to the goat. The postman arrived at the stile. "Alfie, come down a minute, mother called. "Our goat is caught in the wire." I took John and Beattie by the hand and followed a short distance behind. Alfie took his coat off, rolled up his shirt sleeves and knelt by Daisy. "Poor old thing, she is caught by the udder, Mrs Welsh." "What will I do Alfie? It will be some time before the vet gets here. We will have to try and release her and get the bleeding stopped." Aggie came to his aid. As soon as he got Daisy free from the jagged wire, she thrust the linen under her and between them they tied her as firmly as they could. The poor old goat was so shocked and exhausted she did not seem to care when they lowered her to the ground and wrapped her in a rug. "I don't understand how this happened," said mother looking sternly at me. "You were all outside long enough and it's funny none of you heard her." I was certain that the Kane boys and I must look guilty. I thought maybe this was God's punishment for us throwing sods at Johnny Hill.

It seemed ages before the vet arrived but he had been over at Henry Niblock's[1] tending to a horse down with inflammation. "Is she bad?" mother asked anxiously. The vet did not answer until he had properly examined Daisy and by then John Woodside had arrived too.

"One of her teats is almost severed. I will have to give an injection and then stitch her up."

The men carried Daisy into the outhouse and mother went to prepare boiling water. Afterwards the vet said. "I think she will be all right. It was a good job you got her tied up. Send for me again if you're anxious." Mother offered tea but the men would not stay. I saw her take out her last pound to pay the vet. "And Alfie, I don't know how to thank you - oh no, look at the blood on your uniform!" Alfie Jackson laughed, "the Post Office will probably sue you, Mrs Welsh. But I am glad I was behind with my delivery today and was here to help you." "John, I owe you a lot. What would a body do without a good neighbour?"

"That's what neighbours are for, Mrs Welsh. I will come over a wee run before bedtime to see how the old girl fares."

At bedtime father brought mother in to see Daisy. She was lying in the warm straw heated by water bottles. When she saw mother she attempted to get up, but mother knelt down and soothed her. "Poor old girl. Oh Davie, she looks queer," she said anxiously.

"So would you, if you had an accident and an injection. Go and get the gruel and try her with it, Maggie." When I brought in the gruel I could see Daisy look at me pitifully with her green eyes, as if she was saying sorry for all the past antagonism between us.

"Davie, she is sipping it." mother said delightedly. "I don't care if she never gives another drop of milk, as long as she is spared to graze again." "And I don't care as long as she doesn't chase me again," I muttered. Mother chased me out with the towel she had over her arm.

One evening the following week, mother slipped over to see Mrs Kane[2]. She had never been well since the birth of her last child, another boy. In about an hour mother returned. She actually reeled up against the door as she came in, her face the colour of death. "Mrs Kane is dead!" she threw herself into the nearest chair and covering her face she sobbed aloud. The three of us ran to comfort her. "What happened, mother?" Aggie asked gently, putting both arms around her. "We were having our wee cup of tea and her husband Willie arrived home from his boat. "You must have got a wisp of the teapot, Billy," she laughed. She was sitting on the armchair and I had been congratulating her on looking so well. Suddenly, like a crack of your finger, she gave a sigh and fell back and we knew she was gone. I never expected it. Oh wasn't it a mercy that Willie had arrived. I ran for Maggie Johnston[3] and May and then looked for the boys. I met them coming from Tom Ross's. The poor, poor darlings and poor Robert. He nearly went mad." Here mother sobbed anew and we all cried as if our hearts would break. "Five motherless little boys and the youngest only a baby. What is to become of them?" Mother rocked to and fro in her grief and when father came in he couldn't take his tea. They left together to go to the bereaved home and comfort Willie and the boys. We children were subdued all evening. Life was not such a wonderful thing as I had hitherto believed. A dreadful thought struck me, supposing it had been my own darling mother! In the following weeks I did my utmost to surround her with love and care.

Chapter 13
The Great World War

Click clack, click clack,
See our needles fly.
Thinking of our soldier lads
who will conquer or will die.
When far away in battle zone,
Or in Flanders fields they roam,
We will knit them socks
to send with love,
From home, sweet sweet home.

 "Stop!" Mrs Douther's imperious voice sounded like a thunder bolt as she struck the desk sharply with her ruler. "Maggie Welsh, look at those needles of yours, entirely devoid of stitches." She approached where I was standing in line round the piano with the other girls and snapped the sock from my hands. "Disgraceful! Look at the others and at your sister's. Socks neat and stitches complete. Yours looks like a lampshade!" She held it high and the whole class roared with laughter. (It looked awful, right enough.) "God help the poor soldiers or sailors who would be depending upon you!" She picked up the fallen stitches and tried to get it into shape. "This is your last chance. I shall soon have no alternative but to take you out of the act."

I tried my utmost to do better, but found it oh so hard to sing and knit at the same time. How Mollie and the other girls could do it was beyond me. I was glad when Mrs Douther said we would do the Nurses act, which suited me much better. As I put on my nurse's cap and apron I decided that I looked quite lovely with my fair frizzy hair. "Ready girls, good." said Mrs Douther, beginning to conduct our singing, with Elizabeth Dick[1], a senior girl, playing the piano.

We mend them, we tend them,
We cheer them with a smile.
We tell them pleasant stories
Long hours to beguile.
And many a worsted warrior
Up breathes a fervent prayer,
God bless our Red Cross nurses
For all their tender care.

Our practice went on for some time. The boys of Mullaghdubh School were preparing their own act and then we would all join together for the grand finale 'Rule Britannia'. Over a hundred tickets had been sold for the school concert on Friday night. It had been great fun practicing all week and for once being allowed to wear our hair in cloth ringlets so as to look nice for the big night.

For two years now the Great World War had been raging between Germany and Britain. Islandmagee could be proud of the part that she had already played. She had given the cream of her young men by land and sea, particularly at sea. Their courage and devotion to duty was known the world over. They had responded nobly to their country's call and had not flinched in the face of great danger. Many had paid the supreme sacrifice and only a few days ago Samuel Caldwell[2] of the Lang Dale had been lost in the English Channel, his ship the 'SS Teelin Head', sunk by enemy action. He had left a wife and six young children.

'SS Teelin Head' in port. Four Islandmagee mariners, including Samuel Caldwell of Lang Dale, were lost when she was torpedoed in 1918.

A Memorial obelisk to Walter Newel and Billy Edwards still stands overlooking the Gobbins Shore in 2014. It reads - To the memory of Lance Corporal Walter Newel – 6th Batt. Black Watch who fell in action in France on 10/7/1915. Erected by his friends with whom he spent many happy days at the Gobbins farm. On base – Capt. W V Edwards – Royal Dublin Fusiliers, killed in action in Palestine 29/12/1917.

Mother was afraid every night to take up the paper. She sorrowed with the bereaved as if their tragedy was hers. The university boys had all joined up and one of them, Walter Newel[3], had already been killed overseas. Mother cried as if her heart would break. "Oh Davie, I can see Walter coming over the fields to me swinging his towel, coming in as large as life and do you remember that night he persuaded the boys to sleep out all night on the Gobbin top? I am so glad that I did my best to be a mother to them during their holidays. Little did I think his journey in life was going to be so short." Here her tears fell again. Father had to be stern and tell her that she would only make herself ill. "It is the price that we have got to pay Aggie and all our tears will avail nothing. Be thankful that your own boys are not away at sea yet."

Perhaps it was only natural that the full horror of the war had not effected Mollie or me yet. We were still too young to really understand either its meaning or its terrible price. With so much enemy action taking place at sea, the tides around Islandmagee brought a fair share of spoils bouncing in on the waves. Onions, tins of fruit badly dinged by the buffeting seas, electric bulbs and occasionally a still perfectly sealed chest of tea. When this happened the Coastguards were to be informed, to save disputes, for many eyes watched the coast every day. Big heavy hatches would sometimes be washed up too and it was a race between us and the Hills as to who would get them. Living closer to the beach, they had the advantage. They also had a horse to pull the hatches up. Hatches made splendid burning wood, so we were anxious to get all we could. Going to school that particular morning we noticed dark objects floating in the water. There was a big swell on, possibly more hatches, but sometimes they drifted further out towards Blackhead or Whitehead. "Mollie, if Robert Kane comes to the Lang Dale to stay the weekend with his Aunt Aggie Johnston, we will go down the shore with him when we come home." Mollie nodded. It was sad passing Robert's old home, where everything was now deserted. After their mother's death, the Kane children had been separated with Robert and one brother going to their Aunt Bella in Islandmagee, the others to other aunts.

The day before Robert was leaving he had called when we were at tea. Robert looked different somehow, older and more grownup. "Auch hallo, Robert, come on in." Mother was delighted to see him. "There is still a wee drop in the pot. My sisters Mary and Sarah were here yesterday and brought a homemade seed cake. I know it is your favourite. How are things with you?" "Not too bad. I'm going to my Aunt Bella's this week." "Now Robert, isn't it nice that all your family will still be on the Island?" "I know Mrs Welsh, but - I would love to come and live with you. Could you not squeeze me in? I would give as little bother as I could." His anxious, pleading tone was heartbreaking.

"Robert, you know I would love nothing better. Have I not thought of it before myself, but dear, you have to consider your father and respect his wishes also. Your aunts are all fine woman who have their own families and lives. They will be making sacrifices and this will be an upheaval for them too." "You are right, Mrs Welsh. I never thought of that." But when Robert handed me his cup and saucer, he had eaten nothing but a tiny morsel of the seedcake. "Robert, your father promised me that when I get the outhouse roof fixed you can come for long weekends. Davie is going to cement the floor and Tom Browne said he would replace the window and repair the roof. You and the boys can sleep there. So cheer up now, the old happy days are not over." Mother's voice breathed concern and tenderness. I knew she considered Robert like one of her own sons. He had cheered up considerably and looked brighter as he left us.

It was fortunate that Robert was coming for the weekend and we sent him word to meet us immediately after tea. Herby Lynas, who was working over in one of the fields, promised to go to the foot of the Island after tea and get the boys to come home as early as they could. Mollie and I slipped down to the foot of the meadow to see if anything unusual was happening and there was Johnny Hill working away like a mad man. The hatches had

The ruins of Hill's Cottage, still standing at the Gobbins in 2010.

come washing in all right and Johnny had more than he could deal with. He had four or five already slipped up to the tea room, but still had more to shift and it was fast getting dark. Cute as foxes, we crouched behind the hedge spying on him. He didn't seem to have any help today, as Annie was not about. It was late autumn now and the tearooms were closed up for the season. Instead of concentrating on the remaining three or four hatches still on the shore, Johnny was attempting to get the hatches over from the tearoom to his house. "If he goes on like this," said Molly, "hopefully he won't have time to get the ones on the shore tonight." We stayed crouched in our cold, cramped hideout. Eventually it looked as if Johnny had tackled enough for one day. We watched as he struggled down the wet slippery path onto the shore. The tides were rougher and the wind getting up. He pulled the remaining hatches high enough to be safe from the incoming tide and then glancing about to see that no one was watching, he covered them up as best he could with loose seaweed, grass and bracken. Then he made his way homewards. "Good," we both cried triumphantly,"those hatches are as good as ours, Johnny."

After tea my brothers, Robert, Mollie and I slipped down over what was known as the fishermen's path, onto the low shore. We more or less rolled down but although dark and very slippery we knew every inch of the path well. It was was now black and cold and the waves roared against the rocks. There were only a few stars visible and the occasional flashing from Blackhead lighthouse. I imagined Johnny's figure appearing out of the darkness and pouncing on us.

We had not reckoned on the magnitude of our task. The three hatches were heavy, slippery with salt water and to drag them in the almost pitch darkness would have sobered the brightest heart. We had to carry them one by one right to the top, often losing more ground by sliding back or falling than we had gained. But eventually we got the three safely up and for a while no one spoke until we got our breath back. We were content, having outwitted Johnny. It was easier to transport the hatches the rest of the way up the field to the old pighouse, where we locked them securely in. We returned to the warm welcome light of our house tired, dirty and absolutely starving. Mother looked up from the book she had been reading to father. I saw her eyes roam over our appearance but she offered no comment and resumed her reading. I think she had an idea what we had been up to.

On Saturday all was quiet below, so we assumed that Johnny could not be sure what had happened to his missing hatches. But on the Sabbath morning Jim was up early to get ready for church. He was always fastidious about his appearance and everything had to be polished spick and span. To help mother he lit the fire and was fetching another shovel of coal from the coalhouse when he was confronted by Johnny Hill. Jim nearly dropped his shovel in fright. Johnny was a middle aged, pale, delicate looking man. One of his shoulders was a little higher than the other and he had a weak, squeaky voice. But today his face was like thunder. "Where are my hatches, you young pup? Come on, where are they?" "We never saw your old hatches or whatever you call them. So off you go."

My brother Davie had come out in his bare feet when he heard the raised voices. "Lies, lies," shouted Johnny. "I spent yesterday looking for evidence and I came across the marks where you pulled the hatches up the fisherman's path." "Marks," here Davie laughed, "possibly they were snail marks you saw." Johnny went really white with anger. "You impudent rascal," he shook his fist at Davie. Mollie and I peeped out from behind the curtains. "Nice upbringing, I must say, stealing other people's property." "Your property? You don't own the shore or what the sea gives up. You better substantiate your evidence before coming here accusing people on the Sabbath day." I pinched Mollie's arm. Good for Davie. I didn't know he had it in him.

"I'm going now, but you haven't seen the last of me, not by a long chalk. I'll have no one getting one over on me, especially a young pup like you!" Johnny Hill turned and stamped off angrily.

Chapter 14
The Letter

Another year had almost slipped by, but the cruel war raged on. It was August and we children were still on our school holidays. My mother was acting strangely again. She had been muttering to herself more than usual and keeping a constant watch for the postman each morning. Yesterday we had seen her with Mary Woodside, their heads together in deep conversation. We would have given anything to hear what was being discussed. But our suspense continued for another two days, while meantime mother cleaned and polished as if her very life depended upon it, as well as catering for the summer visitors.

"Is the King of England coming?" Aggie eventually asked. Mother just gave a wee smile. "He might, so we had better be prepared." And that was all the satisfaction we were going to get!

Wednesday's post saw Mother hasten up to the stile herself. We watched her open it, although the contents seemed small. In a moment she was hurrying back to the house, her face beaming as she handed the letter to Aggie. "I wanted to be certain, girls, before I could spring the news." She stood like an impatient child, waiting for our reaction. Mollie and I read it over Aggie's shoulder.

Dear Mrs Welsh,
Your very gracious invitation is most cordially accepted.
Accompanied by about eleven of my lads, we hope to arrive with you around two o'clock on Saturday afternoon to spend a few hours. I am sorry I cannot make it a full day as you suggested, but you will readily understand that some of these men have not yet recovered from war wounds.
We are looking forward immensely to meeting you and your family.
With many thanks,
I remain,
Faithfully yours,
Captain JB Brown Riggs.

"It means, girls, that on Saturday we are having eleven wounded soldiers from the UVF Hospital[1] in Belfast." Mother's voice shook and in sheer pleasure she kept wringing her hands together. "And will you charge anything?" I asked. As I spoke I actually stepped back, certain that I would have my ears boxed for impudence. "I should think not indeed. Did you not read the letter properly?" "What made you think of it," Aggie asked, with tenderness in her voice. "Oh, it was the dear university boys and others too. I thought if only I could do something in memory of them. One of their comrades is still spared. He was just beginning to accompany the boys to the Gobbins when war broke out. With Mrs Woodside's help I wrote to him and he sent me Captain Brown Rigg's address. I am going to boil a ham and we will slice it nice and thick and cook it perfectly to keep in the juices. I will also make my potted meat and a little apple sauce and chutney." "No one in the world can make potted meat like you, mother," I said. "I feel hungry just talking about it." "It takes the best shin beef and you must use the jelly bones." And with that, mother bustled away to begin her welcome plans for the visitors.

Saturday arrived, a sunny August day. After an early shower the sun had come up and now our house, surrounded by the whin covered hills, looked such a picture. My beloved Gobbins had never seemed so lovely. Even the cliffs seemed to rise majestically to the occasion, to give as much pleasure as possible to our visitors. Soft easy chairs had been provided by Mrs Woodside and a few more individual chairs and a sofa placed out in the field where the wonderful views could be enjoyed. Across the field could be seen the holiday home where the Newel boys had stayed so happily a few summers past. On a small table cigarettes and sweets had been laid out. But a peep into our tearoom was also rewarding. Mother's best linen draped the big long table with gleaming silver and fresh flowers in vases. There were countless plates of homemade bread: soda, wheaten, potato, oaten and sweet fruit soda. Lovely fresh country butter and home made preserves.

It was an exciting moment when our special guests were spotted in the distance; even wee John was dressed in his best. My mother could certainly rise to the occasion when it demanded and so could father. He could keep quite calm and cool and I believe he could have held his own with the King of England[2]. Both were in their Sunday best clothes, mother in silk blouse and skirt and father in his good suit. We were instructed to keep in the background.

Captain Brown Riggs soon set us all at ease with his warm, friendly manner. He beamed on us all, to express his pleasure. Although not a tall man, he was broad shouldered and possessed a very becoming moustache and the nicest brown eyes imaginable. His voice was clear, with the authoritative tone of his vocation. But the lads, so many wounded in some way. Arms in slings, one blind in an eye, bandaged heads, one on a crutch, another with only one arm. Only a few appeared uninjured. It was shocking to see how the war had ravaged these men, who looked ridiculously young in their blue uniforms. Aggie, Mollie and I felt shy and almost tongue tied. Mother herself was being careful not to display too much emotion.

Most of the boys were content to rest in the sun that afternoon, enjoying the peace and beauty of their surroundings. Except for the occasional drone of an aeroplane in the sky and the wounds these men bore, it was hard to

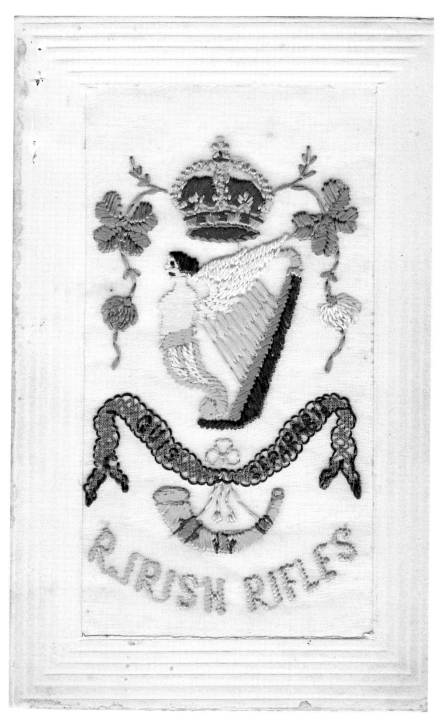

A silk Christmas Card sent from France by an Islandmagee soldier in the Royal Irish Rifles to his family, during the First World War.

believe that a cruel war still raged. One of them, with mother's help, told the group of the happy times spent at Gobbins Farm with comrades now lost. Then in a lighter vein, mother related Willie Holmes's mad enterprises. They seemed to enjoy this and it was good to hear their carefree laughter. Mollie and I had already fallen in love. I could scarcely take my eyes off a tall thin faced lad with a bandaged head who was lying on the grass playing with wee John. Mollie said hers was one with curly hair. He did not have any obvious wounds but we were told he was suffering from shell shock.

"Mrs Welsh, will you sing for us, please?" Captain Brown Riggs asked. "Someone has been giving secrets away," mother laughed, "probably my old man." But there was no nonsense about mother, she did not pretend to be coaxed, but cleared her throat and began to sing.

'As I was a walking one morning in May
A lovely young lass came passing my way.
With cheeks red as roses she sweetly did sing
A bonny blue handkerchief tied under her chin.
"Join in the chorus now boys."
Tied under, tied under,
Tied under her chin.
With a bonny blue handkerchief
Tied under her chin.'

The strong manly voices echoed around the cliffs and whin hills. The applause was deafening when she finished. By this time I had moved nearer to the object of my attraction and when he smiled at me I thought I was in heaven. I noticed that Aggie and one of the other lads were already chatting away as if they were old friends. My progress was slower. "Ernie, it is your turn now." One of the soldiers pushed his friend forward.

I heard the captain whisper softly to my father, "shrapnel wounds in the back, but he returns to the front next week. He has a lovely wife and daughter."

Just before the battle mother
I am thinking most of you.
While upon the hill we're watching
With the enemy in view.
Comrades brave around me lying
Filled with thoughts of home and God.
Full well they know that on the morrow
Some will sleep beneath the sod.

Oh I long to see you mother
And the loving ones at home.
But no I will not leave my banner
Until in honour I can come.
Farewell mother you may never
Press me to your heart again.
But I know you will not forget me mother
If I am numbered with the slain.

The young soldier's rich tenor voice thrilled our hearts but oh the words, it was impossible to curb our emotions, and as for mother, the singer had to gather her close to his heart. "Don't cry, my dear lady. Please God, we will come back again after we have rooted out the enemy to the very last man!"

Someone began to sing 'Keep The Home Fires Burning' and mother made her escape, signaling us to follow her to help with the tea. And what a tea it was! The captain said grace and the men tucked in with great gusto. The bread plates soon had to be refilled and the potato bread disappeared like magic. I doubt they had ever eaten such tasty ham or such delicious potted meat. Conversation and laughter flowed freely. Captain Brown Riggs described it as 'the meal of a lifetime'! The doxology and God Save the King were sung and then finally it was three cheers for their host and hostess, with everyone joining to sing, 'For she's a jolly good fellow'.

Farewells had to be made, but not before some photographs were taken. I had edged myself into the group as near as I could to my young soldier. But my hopes were dashed when I overheard him talk to his pal about "my wife Helen". A few weeks later a photograph appeared in the local paper with the words.

'A group of wounded soldiers with their Captain, JB Brown Riggs, who were very hospitably entertained by Mr and Mrs Welsh of the Gobbins, Islandmagee'.

Chapter 15
The Parting

My school days were over at last. I would never have to worry again about wretched drawings or the horrible canvas schoolbag. Still, it had been a faithful friend, remaining strong and steadfast to the end.

Strangely, I did not feel overexcited about my new freedom. I was a bit apprehensive as to what the future held for me. Mother had been firm. "I'm sorry Maggie, but I could not possibly afford to send you to Belfast to learn shorthand and typing. In the summer months you can help me out with the tearooms and Aggie can stop on in town, but in the winter months you will have to get a job." We had quite an argument about it. Housework appeared to be my only alternative. Weary of pleading and sick of heart, I gave in. But I was determined it would be of short duration, for surely life had something better in store for me? My only consolation was that I would see more of my chum Mary Teare[1], who had left school at the same time and had been employed as a housemaid to Edward Smith[2] in his big house at Browns Bay, at 'the foot of the Island'. I was going to work for his brother Charles B. Smith,

'Cragoran', Charles B Smith's house overlooking Browns Bay, where Maggie Welsh worked as a housemaid about 1920. A grandson, also Charles, lives here today.

who lived in a grand house just opposite. "Oh well," I thought, "I can bear anything for the winter, as long as there is the sure prospect of me going home in the summer to mother and my beloved Gobbins."

I got myself a bicycle and could come home quite frequently. I had attended my first dance at Islandmagee Orange Hall[3]. It looked like the winter might be exciting after all. I would have lots to tell Mollie, who still had two more years to go at school. The lure of the outside world was hard to resist and for a time I forgot about my minister's wise counsel about 'green pastures', Harry Benson and the mission hall people and Edna Whyte away in the mission field.

On one of my afternoons off in early November, I noticed mother was looking very tired. She seemed to have lost weight and had not her usual good colour. Mollie was away to Whitehead with Jeannie Caldwell. I gathered up all the ironing and put the flat irons on the red fire. As usual, Beattie and wee John were playing together. Mother had a fire going in the tea house and she sat knitting with Snowball stretched out on the fender. I was telling her all my news. She seemed pleased that I felt more settled. The door suddenly opened and Jack Kane stood in the threshold. He had been one of those fortunate Island men who had escaped the ravages of war.

I should have told my readers that the four years of the Great War were now over. Islandmagee in particular could hold her head high. Sorrow had developed into a calm resignation and a fierce pride that not only had their men resolutely answered their country's call, but in the thick of the fight, on land and particularly at sea, had displayed such devotion to duty that they had won the admiration of the world.

"Come in, Jack," mother said so sharply, that I looked up at her in surprise. Jack Kane looked ill at ease, standing somewhat awkwardly, twisting his cap in his hand. "You have no need to tell me why you are here Jack. You are for marrying Jane McClarnon from the Red Brae in a few weeks and you want wee John back." "News seems to have travelled fast, Agnes Welsh, but that is the sum and substance of it. Jane thinks it would be better if the children were together." "Jane thinks, so Jane thinks! A fat lot she knows about it! Did she take him when he was lying at death's door? Did she walk the floor night and day for months when the whole world seemed to me to be sleeping and I was alone with an ailing infant in my arms keeping a constant vigil night after night? Did she ever see the wonderful moment when his crying ceased, when soon his little eyes would smile up at me and then the first day when his little arms encircled my neck calling me "Mammy," for the first time? When I watched with such pride his first little footsteps coming slowly but surely toward me. And now you come wanting him again, but by the heavens above, I will not part with my little John!"

She fled without a word of warning, returning again fiercely hugging John in her arms, her sobs shaking them both. John showed little interest in his father. He smiled at the woman he knew as mammy as if he thought it was silly for her to cry. "Mammy, don't cry. When I am a big boy next week I am for going for a bag of flour with Donald." The little voice with its tender tone only added to her sorrow. "Please Aggie, don't distress yourself." Jack Kane put his hand on mother's shoulder. I left down the flat iron and took John from her. Mollie had returned. I whispered it all to her and tenderly we made mother sit down. "I feel like a brute to inflict this sorrow upon you, Aggie. Don't think that I am indifferent. It has been no easy matter for me to come here today on a mission such as this. I am only too aware of the extent of your sacrifice and your labour of love for my child. I cannot ever repay you, I cannot express even in the merest words the debt I owe or my regards for you, Aggie Welsh. I can only say this, the good God above knows all and he will reward you richly. I have been criticised for getting married again but I feel a lost lonely person. Life at sea is hard enough sometimes, God knows, but it is infinitely worse to come home to an empty house, especially now my mother is gone. I envy those with happy families and comfortable homes. Jane McClarnon is a fine woman and she has been lonely herself. Don't think that we did not consider you. As a woman she knew what this would mean to you. We wanted to spare you if we could, but we had to consider the other children. What would be nicer than brother and sister growing up together and I could not evade my duty to my son. It is going to be hard for us both and also for John to make this break, but I hope you can understand that it would become more difficult the longer the matter is postponed."

My mother had now composed herself. "Say no more Jack. The fault lies with me. The child's proper place is in his own home. It was me who came to you and pleaded to take him. I must not forget that. It's comforting to know your future wife wants you all to be together. It is a good clear index of her character. But Jack, I am determined that the upheaval in wee John's life must be gradual. He could start by going for a day with you to get used to your home. After all, my wee darling will only be a short distance away from me along the low shore." It was heartbreaking to see mother trying to convince herself and bravely trying to look on the bright side. Jack sat down beside her at the fire and I could see concern and sympathy in his face and voice. "Whatever you say, Aggie," he said hoarsely, "I will fall in with whatever you suggest."

Then a queer look came over mother's face that puzzled me. "There is something else, Jack, that I must tell you about." She looked over to where Mollie and I were finishing off the ironing. "Girls, leave the ironing for now and go and look after the children in the upper house." We reluctantly had to obey. Mother did not want us to hear the rest of their conversation.

Mollie and I argued because I wanted to waylay Jack as he left and plead with him to let us keep wee John. "It's no use," Mollie cried, choking on her tears, "you will only annoy the man and mother will be furious." But eventually she allowed me to go, saying, "well I cannot go with you, as mother needs one of us here."

I waited for Jack Kane near Hill's Teahouse. It was a dull day and the rain was not long over. It would soon be November but I saw none of my surroundings. My heart was too heavy. Jack came at last, slipping and sliding on the wet dirty path. I tried to plead my cause, but my stammering seemed both inadequate and my cause hopeless. "I don't know if I should be telling you this, Maggie," he said. "I only know that it is a wise thing to bring John home again in the face of what your mother has just told me. Perhaps it will soften the blow for you all if your energies and concern should be centred now on your mother." I stared at him, not understanding his meaning. "Maggie, your mother is not too well. She says it it nothing serious, but her heart has being playing her some queer tricks. She had to get the doctor one day when she was alone. He said she must rest more and if she followed his advice she would be all right. Can you see Maggie that it's wiser for me to take back my full responsibility for John." I was stunned. Mother had said nothing, not even to father, I guessed. Jack tried to reassure me. "Remember, there's nothing to worry about, your mother will be able to get a bit of rest now the winter is here and if you tell the others in confidence, you can all help her get the care and attention she needs."

His words sounded plausible, but a deep suspicion was lurking in my heart. She was failed and somehow I knew that. "Thank you for telling me, Jack. I'll talk to my sister Nellie. She's the eldest and between us we will keep a stricter eye on mother." But in that moment I felt a terrible helplessness, a sense that my carefree days of childhood had disappeared forever and I had crossed over to the responsibilities and problems of adulthood.

I will not dwell too much on our family's sad parting from wee John Kane. One afternoon, a few weeks later, Mollie and I took John to his father and new mother. The new Mrs Kane received us in a friendly fashion, but she made no extra effort to befriend John. She was not a bad looking woman with nice curly dark hair, tall and perhaps a little over forty. I could not decide how I felt about her. John's mother Mary Kane had been soft and gentle-natured, but his stepmother seemed more direct and businesslike. I expect I was prejudiced and judged her more harshly, believing that she was responsible for causing my mother so much sorrow. How prone we are to judge, so certain that we are right at the time. The new Mrs Kane would have her own sorrows within a short time. Her own little baby girl, a beauty with a lovely head of curls, died shortly after her first birthday. Only a few brief years later, Mrs Kane followed her infant daughter, leaving Jack Kane a widower again. But she had been good to her step children and a great worker, setting Jack back on his feet again.

As usual, I am wandering away from my present story, dipping into the future instead. John had been running out and in to Grace in the shed where she was making bubbles with an old clay pipe. He was fascinated but came in occasionally to make sure we were still there. The day was beginning to fall. "Run for it now!" Jack Kane said after John had returned to Grace another time. Mollie and I looked at each other. "Oh dear God, not this," we felt like screaming. But we obeyed and took to our heels, past the back of the shed, down over the field and onto the low shore. Then we stopped and listened. Thank God, not a sound in the still November evening, only the gentle lap of waves on the beach. But suddenly it came. John shrieking his heart out - "Mollie, Maggie!" screaming our names into the air. The cries continued but grew fainter; they had probably taken him indoors by then. We ran stumbling on with tears our only company. We stopped near Johnny Hill's and tried to get our story right for our parents. We didn't want our precious mother any more upset so we told a white lie. I think we played our parts well, for we came home smiling. "Oh mother, it worked out fine. John got on so well with his sister and he was having so much fun with the bubbles..." But mother turned and faced us. "How did you leave him?" Her eyes never left us. Mollie replied calmly without hesitating, "we slipped away while he was playing with Grace and we heard not a sound. Mrs Kane was getting a nice tea ready and Jack had a lovely red wheelbarrow for John, (this last part was true)."

Mother's lip trembled, but then she smiled. "Thank God the sorrows of childhood are not long lived. God in his mercy hath willed it."

If our mother was putting on an act similar to our own, she did it well. Jim and Davie had arranged to come home early and they arrived just when we needed them most. Mother's eyes brightened up at the sight of her two sons. Their coming dispersed the sadness. "I have my family," she whispered proudly, "and my husband; many a woman is bereft of all. It is a sin for me to rebel at this will of God. I did my duty by the motherless boy, so let me be content to leave it there."

Chapter 16
Letter From New York

There was great rejoicing when my eldest sister's baby was announced. It was a proud and happy moment when mother held her first grandchild, a darling little boy, in her arms. Nellie had married a fine man working for the Belfast Corporation and they had set up home in Belfast. "God's love and mercy is over us all," mother would repeat often as she proudly nursed her grandson. I think it helped to compensate her for the loss of wee John who she always talked about. His father seldom had time to bring him to see her now. He had said on one occasion that it was better for the parting to be a complete break. And although I think it was with a heavy heart, mother had not pressed him to change his mind. "It is his wife now who rules the roost, for Jack is away so much at sea," she would say. The new grandchild also helped to soften the blow of my brothers Jim and Davie both going off to sea. Recently a letter had come saying they had left their ship in New York to seek work there. I was glad that I had not been at home when it had arrived, for my parents had had too many losses to bear in recent times. The death of their neighbour, Robert's mother, the loss of so many loved ones in the Great War and the parting of their dearest wee John had hit them hard. Also, my little sister Beattie had developed polio at only seven years of age. The only known remedy for it in those days was to carry up salt water, heat it and bathe the affected parts with the water and pieces of seaweed. Fortunately it was only her legs that were affected but for a considerable time she could not walk. But gradually life returned to her limbs and she could later walk with only a slight limp. Beattie married and went to Australia where she lives today with her lovely family of six.

My parents had missed the boys sorely, for they always waited patiently for their boat to come in and mother would watch out the window until she saw them leap over the stile with their canvas sailor's bags over their shoulders. Jim had the softest heart of the two, and when he had to leave to join his ship he would fight to keep the tears away, waving and waving until he was out of mother's sight. Johnny Hill had also passed away recently after only a few days illness, and believe it or not both my parents felt sad about it.

I have often thought that it is strange how natural forces that play such an important part in our lives for a time, will continue long after we are gone. We try to control them, but they are really beyond human control. The same well which caused so much friction between the Hills and my parents still flows to this day, while they are long dead and their homesteads deserted. Such is nature and such is life.

The letter from New York was given to me to read one day on my afternoon off. I was puzzled as to why my brothers took this course, for I thought they loved their home and parents dearly. But the letter explained. "Mother dearest, we are not just thinking of ourselves," Jim wrote. "The pay for a deckhand is not much these days. We honestly thought of you, slaving away in the tearooms and making so little, for you are too generous, feeding the multitudes and not making any profit. We also considered father slaving away at the old quarry, particularly on cold bad days. You may have heard that Bob Heddles[1] got a splendid job here. He came aboard our ship and convinced us to make the break and try our luck here. Fortunately we got work within a week. I am operating the lift in one of the big giant skyscrapers with an excellent starting wage and Davie has got started in a glass factory. Bob Heddles could not get us lodgings with him, but his landlady put us in touch with a Mrs Baker. It seems she has a shine for the Irish boys. (Or perhaps it is because I am so good looking?) Her grandparents came from Limerick. She has a big Irish heart and she is already like a mother to us. But no dear, not quite. Nobody can ever take your place. Oh mother mine, you are the dearest person in my life," (here the letter had been blotted as if some tears had been shed), "so please don't be sad, mother darling and father. All is well and we are well cared for. This great city of New York is very exciting but we are also aware of all the dangers. We shall try, with God's help, not to stray from the path that you and father directed us on from early childhood. We hope to make you proud and never ashamed of us. With our first weeks pay we have managed to buy you some nice glassware for the kitchen cabinet. Securely packed by the shop keeper himself and with a final go over by Mrs Baker, it is on its way to you."

Despite the cheery optimistic letter, our hearts ached for our absent loved ones, fearing that we might never see their faces again. Sadly, my darling mother never did. It was only after her death that Davie came home for good but Jim could not bear to see our home without her and he returned to New York for good.

The new baby, as I have said, was mother's salvation. She had been ill and broken hearted after the letter from the boys. So much that the Rev Steen came to offer help and comfort. He had had some success. His imitation of an American accent had made mother smile. She managed to pick up the threads of her life again. The old family cradle which had rocked us all, including wee John, was brought out again for the new arrival. "You could have him all summer mother, if you feel equal to it," Nellie had said. "I could then go back to work in the fruit shop, as an extra bit of money is not to be despised, but if you feel that's too much, perhaps the occasional weekend?"

The parcel from my brothers eventually arrived. By then I was employed as a housemaid at Smith's of Browns Bay, which I had no great liking for.

Mollie told me that it took some time to unearth the treasure from amongst wood shavings and layers of paper. Half a dozen lovely amber coloured glasses with a design of pink roses, a jug to match and two fruit dishes. Inside an envelope were written, 'To the dearest mother and father', with dollars to the value of £2. Father insisted the money should go to buy a new mat for the hearth, to match the splendour of our new china.

A few weeks later old Sam Duff arrived with the coal. Yes, he was still surviving, but was now very 'doddery' on his feet. He could no longer unload or load the coal himself, but his boss and his customers seemed willing to do the work. I should have told you reader, that Belinda had died a few years back. She had fallen from her roost and mother found her lying peacefully on the ground. We all shed tears at her passing and then Daisy had followed soon after. She was very old and had long ceased to give milk. I actually felt sorry because she had, in her way, played a prominent part in my life. Old Sam was still wearing his battered green hat. He started to come in, then hesitated. "Boy, oh, boy, Mrs Welsh, I thought I was stepping into Buckingham Palace. I had better take off my boots." "Don't you dare," Mollie had replied quickly. "We would not relish the odour." Sam's face fell, believing she was serious and in remorse she spontaneously kissed his old weatherbeaten cheek. "Love begets love, Mrs Welsh," he had wheezed. "I knew Mollie was worth waiting for." "Fair enough, Sam," laughed mother. "In future I will be looking for my coals for nothing, if you are going to be one of the family."

Chapter 17
The Day is Ended

I was in tremendous spirits. My eighteenth birthday was approaching and soon I would be leaving Smith's at Browns Bay for good and going home to help mother for the summer months. I would miss the dances in the Orange Hall, where my chum Mary Teare and I had had such great times and I had made the pleasant discovery that some young men were interested in my company. Not to the same extent as Mary or my sister Mollie, but I was not passed by as in earlier days, so this cheered me immensely. I would have no time in the summer months to enjoy myself in this fashion and I knew right well that mother preferred that I did not attend such places.

Islandmagee Orange Hall, where Maggie Welsh went to her first dances, was built in 1876 on Whitish Hill, Ballypriormore townland by the local Orange Lodge 1962.

At times I did think of Harry Benson and his Christian group and often Edna Whyte's face would loom up before me. Even Willie Holmes would lecture me when I chanced to meet him. Within me something kept whispering, "you are wasting a young promising life on the vain, paltry things of the world that cannot bring joy." There was a battle going on within me. Life at this age seemed so exciting, but was it life with a capital 'L'.?

For the time being, I put such thoughts aside. My greatest joy at the moment was that I was going home for good to my dear parents and beloved Gobbins. Mother had been unwell for part of the winter and spring. After a visit from Dr Dundee she had told us it was just a bit of a heart complaint, nothing to worry about she had insisted vehemently. If she was careful and rested a lot, all would be well. My father was concerned and had tried to quiz her further, but she had just laughed and told him to have a bit of sense. Since then, she had taken several weak turns from which she appeared to have recovered.

I had not seen her for over a week and when I arrived home that day I was shocked by her appearance. She looked a ghost of her former self, her eyes sunken in her face and I was certain she was in considerable pain. I was afraid to alarm father, until he said he been over several times to John Woodside's at night for a taste of whiskey for her and he and John had sat with her through a particularly bad night, propping her up high with pillows when she could not get a breath and her palpitations were severe. Mollie and I vowed we would nurse her back to health. We would do all the work and we were both capable now of doing the cooking as well. But mother would not hear of us sending yet for Agnes, or to alarm Nellie about her.

Only a short time later, on a lovely early June morning with the whins alive with colour and birdsong and the perfume of roses in the air, my angel mother passed away into the house of the Lord forever. Such a beautiful summer day, just the sort that my mother would always have greeted with, "it's great to be alive on a day like this." Now she was unaware of it, having been very ill for the last week and lapsing in and out of consciousness. The tea room had had to be closed. Nellie and Agnes had been sent for, and along with father and some of mother's sisters, we had never left mother's bedside. One particular night when the going had been hard, father had stayed beside her all night. "Even though I walk through the valley of the shadow of death, I shall fear no evil." She had stirred and slowly opened her eyes. "Is the going hard, Agnes?" The perspiration was streaming down her face and Nellie wiped her cheeks and brow. Mother nodded her head. "Joy cometh soon," she whispered with much effort, and her eyes closed again. If my mother had been living in the present age, with so many wonderful drugs now to alleviate the pain of heart disease, we would not have seen her suffer so greatly and her passing could have been so much easier.

In the following few days our house became crowded with relatives and friends. The Field Club members, friends from the Mission hall, Harry Benson and countless more. Jack Kane and his wife, with wee John[1], were

Entrance to the Gobbins, Islandmagee.

Photo,50368, Coon, Moira

After the death of Mrs Agnes Welsh in 1924, the family closed their tearoom. It was not until 1926 that a newly built 'Gobbins Cafe and Tearooms', was built by Tom Browne, just beside the cottage. Mrs Browne ran the tearooms for a while and a Mr Kane had tearooms in 1935.

among the first to arrive to pay their respects. Jack said little, but sometimes silence is more eloquent than words. As he gripped father's hand in his and expressed his deepest regrets, I noticed his lips tremble. The anguish in my father's face was pitiful to behold. I had to turn away. Once he stumbled from her bedside and cried out in a broken voice. "How am I going to bear the days without her?" Wee John was crying his heart out. Although now a boy of six, he could still remember his time with my mother and realise that she was gone. She had been his mother when he had known no other and they had spent many happy hours together with her cuddling him in her arms. "Oh mother," I whispered sadly to myself, "if you could only see John now, you would know how deeply the wee fellow loved you and how rewarding was your care and sacrifice for him." It was Agnes who took John by the hand and led him away to play with my sister's baby.

Members of the Field Club came to pay their respects to the woman who had been their hostess for so many years. Now the future of Welsh's tearooms lay in the balance. Certainly things would never be the same again. In my own sorrow I had cried out fiercely, "God has taken away my mother and I shall hate him forever. I am leaving home and the Gobbins for good and I never want to see it again!" But Aunt Mary, one of mother's sisters, rebuked me." Maggie, you must pull yourself together and face life resolutely. Your duty is now to your father and young sister. Your father's loss is greater than yours, for he has lost his life's companion. He will not be able to pick up the threads of his life so easily. You are young, your life is before you. And what about your brothers away in a foreign land? The news will stagger them. You must help to soften that blow, Maggie. Let them know that as a loving family you are sticking together. Your desertion of duty could have a far reaching effect on their lives, far from home in a city of temptation. Ask yourself the question, what would my mother have me do, and you will know the answer. Consider Robert Kane, bereft of a mother, with four younger brothers. He was not as fortunate as you, having had no sisters to support him. His baby brother had no precious recollections of his mother. Maggie, you are a young woman now, able to fend for yourself and just think of the store of golden memories you will have of your mother. Robert faced his ordeal well and it is up to you to do the same."

At that moment I could not follow my Aunt's wise advice, for I was engulfed in a fierce rebellious anger. My precious mother was dead and my world toppled in ruins at my feet. I was only human and I am ashamed to say that my angry rebellion lasted for some time and caused much heartache to my dear father. My eighteenth birthday, which I had been so eagerly looking forward to in the next few weeks - now I did not care if I ever saw it! Looking back I realise that my sisters' sorrow must have been as great as mine, but they had greater strength of character and admirable restraint. But God in his gracious love and mercy did not desert me. Even in my darkest hour he led me to an unexpected new friend, almost out of the blue. They helped me to dry my tears and made my birthday, if not exactly a happy one, at least free from angry rebellion and more able to accept the sorrow which we all have to face sometime in our lives.

A group of young men from McQuiston Mission Hall had come to camp in John Woodside's barn for the July holiday. On their first day they stopped on their way to the Gobbins Path to offer their sympathy for our loss. One of them had visited before and knew our parents. The tallest one of the group, to my amazement, was interested in my company. He was a Queen's University student and intending to enter the Presbyterian Church. He became a friend and a tower of strength to me. On the day of my birthday party, which father allowed us to have in the tearoom, I invited him and the other lads along. They insisted on bringing their own food. We had a quiet, dignified tea with my sisters, father and the boys. We sang a hymn, had a prayer, and of course there were tears, but now they had lost much of their bitterness. For more than fifty years, that young man, who became the Reverend Thomas R Johnston[2], has been my unfailing friend.

Once again my great love of nature was aroused from the depths of apathy. Could I really have said I hated the Gobbins and all its beauty? Ah no, and I was ready to take up my pen once more. I had found not only

The steep, winding path that led from Welsh's cottage down to the Gobbin's shore.

healing, but through a grievous cross the Creator of all nature had become inexpressibly dear to me. And as I began to walk in 'green pastures', so nature now assumed an even deeper and richer meaning for me . My new friendship made me both proud and humble. I tried to act as I had been instructed by my aunt and on the gracious, spiritual advice given by my new friend. The pain of losing my mother did not disappear, but resigning myself to the will of God helped to make me a better woman and with God's help I was able to face my life without bitterness.

A few weeks later, on a perfect summers evening, Tom Browne was finishing his last field of hay in the meadow. He had plenty of helpers from the young people at Burnside Cottages. Nearby, old Donald, still alive and active, pulled the tumbling paddy[3] which tossed the hay ready to be forked into ricks. Mollie and I were supposed to be helping too, but I am afraid we were not exerting ourselves much. A sharp whistle came from Mrs Woodsides. She was calling Tom and his servant boy for tea. A while back John had married a fine woman from Ballynure and Mary had since married her butcher, Hamilton Quee.

Tom waved back a ready response. "A cup of tea would be very welcome, Herby lad," he had smiled. It was then Mollie noticed a man coming over Johnston's stile. "I am certain it is Mr Davidson from the Field Club, I know his walk," she said. "You are right, Mollie, we had better get home for father is on his own." I called to Beattie, who was having great fun in the hay. Her health now was much improved and she had been left with only a bit of a limp. She had taken after my mother in good looks.

We had left father's dinner on the hob, a pot of pretty unappetising stew, with a note on the door... 'Key in usual place, stew ready'. As I came in the door, hearing the pathetic note in father's voice made me feel guilty and ashamed. "It is changed times, Mr Davidson, to come home from work to a message like that." Father was sitting taking the stew and Mr Davidson had seated himself by the window. He gave us a smile and continued with his conversation. "Once the mother goes, Mr Welsh, everything changes. I am glad in a way that you have decided to close the tearooms. I could not possibly conceive of the business going on without her. She was a wonderful woman with a great personality. It was sheer pleasure to be in her company, never mind her wonderful food. None will miss her more than the Field Club." "There are certainly going to be changes, Mr Davidson. The girls and I have been talking and making decisions. Mollie will stop at home, at least for a bit. I think Beattie and I could manage together. Maggie here will go back to work." "It will take a bit of time for the girls to adjust themselves, Mr Welsh. "They have been sheltered so long and it must be bewildering to find themselves so suddenly adrift." "Sure don't I know it," father smiled. "It is not every man that has five lovely daughters."

Reader, now I understand that my father was proud of us, even when we did not always deserve it, certainly I did not, but the years give us all more wisdom and understanding.

Thank God my father was spared to a ripe old age and that we were there to comfort him in his declining years. Not that he ever complained. He was so bright and cheery and so very independent. Like myself, he loved books and reading and the simple things of life sufficed him. When he eventually passed away, it was at the grand old age of eighty-eight with a smile on his face.

Leaving the table briskly, Father reached up to the mantleboard and handed Mr Davidson a slip of paper. "Why, this is American dollars, Mr Welsh, and quite a bit of money." "It is from my boys. As you know, my wife Aggie idolised them. They have risen to the occasion in a way that would make her so proud." Father almost broke down and I could scarcely keep from throwing my arms around him. "I am delighted for you, Mr Welsh. Tell me, do you know of anyone having a wireless set around here?" "Yes, Willie Holmes has one. I think he's the only one I know. Only those who have money can afford such luxury." "Father, the Woodsides have got one now," Mollie said. "Well Mr Welsh, I shall be here on Monday with a wireless set for you, complete with ear phones. It is a gift from the Field Club members in appreciation of all the services rendered to us by Mrs Welsh and your worthy self. We thought it would be good company for you in the evenings. I know you like good stories and plays." "And all the news, Mr Davidson. Just think of it, sitting in your own armchair and hearing about events from all over the world." Father was not a man who found it easy to display his feelings openly, but the thought of such a gift overwhelmed him. "All I can say to you and your friends Mr Davidson, is thank you and may God bless you for ever and ever."

Reader, I will end now on this happy note and reluctantly bid you farewell, leaving behind my fond childhood memories to rejoin the present world again. Please God, perhaps one day a pen more eloquent than mine will pay a worthy tribute to the wondrous beauty of my beloved Gobbins.

Margaret McBride née Welsh

Appendix 1

What happened to the Welsh family?

David Welsh senior: After his wife Agnes's death, he stayed in Islandmagee, moved to live near his daughter Mollie at Erection Cottages, Ballyharry and died in 1961 in his 89th year. He is buried with Agnes and one child Bessie, who died aged 10 months in 1911, at St Johns COI cemetery, Islandmagee.

Nellie: The eldest child, worked in Turner's Fruit Shop in Belfast. She married Samuel Bennett, a Belfast Corporation employee. They had one baby boy before her mother Agnes Welsh died in 1924 and later another boy.

Jim: He went to sea with his brother Davie. The brothers left their ship and got jobs in in New York but although Davie came back home after his mother died, Jim settled in America, eventually working in security services for a bank. He married Emma and they had no family.

Davie: Settled in Ulster on his return from America, married Mary Ann (May) and had two children David and Gloria. They often stayed at Portmuck and their son David Welsh sang in the Rhinka Ballroom. He was a freelance journalist for local papers and often wrote about Islandmagee people and places. May died in 1986 aged 86. Family are buried in Islandmagee New Cemetery.

Agnes: the fourth child, worked as a nursemaid in Belfast. She had two children Margaret and Cathleen and two grandchildren, Susan and Lawrence. Agnes died in 1994 and is buried in Islandmagee New Cemetery.

Margaret 'Maggie': The fifth child and author of 'Green Pastures'. After her mother died she was 18, she went to live and work in Belfast and later married Andrew McBride. They had two daughters, Doreen and Norah. During the Blitz years, when her husband was at war, Margaret came back to live in Islandmagee for a while. Doreen was actually born in a cottage beside St John's COI. Margaret McBride's grandchildren are: Thomas Andrew, Diane, Ruth, Janet, Linda and Julie. She dedicated 'Green Pastures' to her grandson.

Mollie: was the only Welsh child to settle in Islandmagee, she married Sam Ford, who worked at Ballylumford Power Station. They lived at Erection Cottages, Ballyharry past the New Cemetery. They had three sons,

Norman, Ivan and Aubrey. Ivan had two daughters and a son. The two daughters still live in the area, one at Duff's Corner and one in Larne. Aubrey moved to Larne.

Beatrice (Beattie): the youngest child, recovered from her childhood polio and emigrated to Australia in 1956 where she married and had six children.

About 1972, four surviving Welsh sisters**, Maggie, Agnes, Beattie** and **Mollie** were reunited at the Gobbins.

Appendix 2:
Photographs:

Margaret Welsh McBride with two of her grandchildren Ruth and Diane in 1960s.

David Welsh with his daughter Maggie McBride (baby unknown).

The Welsh Sisters, reunited at the Gobbins c1972.
Maggie, Agnes, Beattie, Mollie (L to R).

David Welsh (centre) at Ballyharry with some his children and grandchildren.

Jim Welsh, Maggie's older brother, with his dogs in New York.

Appendix 3:
Timeline

1901 The Census records the **Welsh** family were renting at 22 Cloughfin, Islandmagee from a **Mary Alexander**. The family then were:
David Welsh 28, Presbyterian, Agricultural Labourer, read and write
Agnes Welsh 28, Wife, read and write
Nellie Welsh 2, Daughter
James Welsh 4 months, Son

May 1901 Construction work began on a two mile coastal cliff path at the Gobbins, designed by **Berkeley Deane Wise**, chief engineer with the Belfast & Northern Counties Railway. Wise's plans linked iron bridges and tunnels with sections of walkways high above the sea to allow access to heights never before scaled and amazing views of the cliffs and coastline that would previously only have been possible from a boat. Steel tubular and suspension bridges were built at Harland and Wolff's yards in Belfast and floated out on barges from Whitehead before being hoisted into position. The first section of the two mile long path opened in **August 1902,** and an advertisement ran proclaiming that the *'New cliff path along the Gobbins Cliffs, with its ravines, bore caves, natural aquariums ... has no parallel in Europe as a Marine Cliff Walk.'*

24 Aug 1902 The **Belfast Naturalists Field Club** were in their 39th year of existence when an excursion was made by about 70 members to the newly constructed Gobbins Path. Those attending included botanists, conchologists, geologists and folk who simply enjoyed an afternoon in the country. About half the party travelled by the 12:50 train to Ballycarry, where they were taken by car to the top of Gobbins Lane where they proceeded on foot to the shore. The group noted that progress, which had been difficult in previous years, was much improved by the stiles and footbridges erected by the Northern Counties Railway at all the difficult areas. The group first visited the 'Smugglers Cave'. Tea was taken at the *'hospitable'* tearooms of Mrs Hill, close beside a *'well-marked'* pathway leading round the foot of the Gobbins cliffs. From here the group were escorted by Mr Berkeley Deane Wise, engineer of the Northern Counties Railway and designer of the new Gobbins Path, until the first series of caves was reached. *'This path has been carried round the foot of the headland well above the high water mark along the ledges of basalt and where walls of rock used to meet the traveller in former visits, he will now find short tunnels cut through solid rock. Where a gaping chasm yawned there is now a hanging bridge constructed of* *bearers of rolled iron girders with a footway of solid plank; even the nervous need not fear to pass, for the sides of the path are furnished with a wire railing to stout uprights of iron, which have a sure foundation deep in the rock'.* The party explored these caves, the more adventurous going in a 'considerable distance' without reaching the end and finding many varieties of lichen, ferns and liverwort. Mr Wise explained to them the Company's intention to continue construction of the path to reach more of the caves, with his plan to ultimately provide access to all further of the seven caves, known as the 'Seven Sisters', along the Islandmagee coastline to Heddles Port.

27 Sept 1903 A particularly large number of the **Belfast Naturalists Club**, 126 members, took part in their final summer excursion to the **Gobbins Cliff Path**, then only opened a year by the enterprise of the Northern Counties Railway. The Vice President **William Fennell** and Hon Sec **Mr Robert Patterson** acted as guides. The large numbers attending meant that cars picking the party up at Ballycarry station had to do double trips, as each car could only carry seven people plus the driver. Assembling near **Hill's Cottage**, the group began the Cliff Path walk together. The botanists discovered examples of sea spleenwort, and species of birds observed included songthrush, blackbird, stonechat, redbreast, wren, pied wagtail, One member of the Club handed in a list of birds he had noticed during the afternoon, which included 24 species. The club were much impressed with the construction and engineering of the Gobbins Path itself,and stated their intention to return to the *'safe structures of Mr Wise the engineer of the railway company'.* On their return the group stopped at **Hill's cottage** for tea. Their large numbers seemed to have caused a problem with food and milk supplies,' *but the resourceful efforts of the Hon. Sec. surmounted all difficulties'* it was reported. *'He foraged around and got in extra provisions, and even when the milk was finished he was not to be beaten for he commandeered a cow and brought it into the camp'.* However, his attempts to get milk from the poor animal seem to have *'caused much amusement'.* The naturalists then returned to Ballycarry via the cars and on to Belfast. *'All agreeing that the final outing of the season had been a great success.'*

May 1904 The Larne Times and Weekly Telegraph of 14 May, reported *The Gobbins Path* open again for the season. ' *The usual improvements rendered essential after the winter storms have been carried out most effectively. The arrangements for conveying tourists to and from the Gobbins are almost complete'.*

1906 Margaret 'Maggie' Welsh, was born in a cottage close to the Gobbins Cliffs at Islandmagee on the County Antrim coast. Her parents were **David**

'Davie' Welsh, originally from Loughmourne near Carrickfergus, who worked as a labourer at Ballylig Limestone Quarry at Magheramorne and Agnes ...?, one of a large Islandmagee family, whom he married about 1897. Maggie Welsh was the fifth of two boys and five girls. Two other children had died in infancy.

The Gobbins had become even more of a popular tourist attraction after a spectacular 'Gobbins Cliff Path', designed by NCR engineer **Berkeley Deane Wise**, was opened in 1902 and Maggie's mother Agnes Welsh had opened a tearoom adjacent to their thatched cottage, known as *Welsh's Tea Rooms*. Unfortunately their close neighbours, **John and Margaret Hill** of Hills Port, had already been running a similar establishment known as Hill's Tearooms, so this caused the souring of good relations between the two families. In 1924 when Maggie's mother Agnes died of heart problems aged only 52, Welsh's Tea Rooms closed. From childhood, Maggie Welsh had always loved to write prose and poetry and over her life she regularly sent her work to local newspapers and magazines. In 1968 one of her poems written about Islandmagee was published in a re-edited version of Dixon Donaldson's 'History of Islandmagee' by **Victor Glenn**, a schoolteacher at Kilcoan School, Islandmagee. On retiring in the 1960's, she was encouraged by her grandchildren to record her childhood memories of the Gobbins and the stories that they enjoyed hearing her tell them and she dedicated this unpublished work, entitled 'Green Pastures,' to her grandson, **Thomas Hamilton**. 'Green Pastures' provides a fascinating and valuable glimpse of what life was like in Islandmagee a hundred years ago. Maggie McBride was living in Carrickfergus when she died aged 69 on the 16 August 1975. She was survived by her children and husband **Andrew**, who passed away in January 1982. They are both buried in Islandmagee New Cemetery.

10 June 1906 120 members and friends of the **Belfast Naturalists** again took the 2:15 train to Ballycarry for their second excursion of the season to the *Gobbins Cliff Path*. Accompanied by their president WH Phillips and secretary George Donaldson their programme included copies of the pamphlet *'The Gobbins Cliff Path'* written by **Mr William J Fennell MRIA** in 1902 for the visit of the British Association when it was officially opened. At Ballycarry the party divided, with half taking cars and the others walking to the Gobbins. The walk *'afforded many opportunities of investigation for the botanists and geologists'*. Wood vetch and adders tongue fern were found *'in great abundance'*. But *'much indignation was felt when it was discovered that sea spleenwort, which Mr Berkeley Wise had taken so much pains to protect, had almost entirely disappeared'*. In the undercliffs near Hill's Port a number of spherical chambers about an inch in diameter clustered together were said to be the winter homes of the common garden snail, which hibernates in the crevices and gradually excavates further in, sometimes imprisoning itself and dying from starvation. Many of the shells remained like bones in a broken tomb and could be seen and felt, an *'interesting phenomenon'* in the rocks close behind 'Hill's Cottage', a *'whitewashed habitation close to the shore.'* At 6 o'clock the naturalists took tea at Hill's Cottage, which, *'although not served with the promptness, nor surrounded with all the desirable accessories of a high-class restaurant, was nevertheless much appreciated.'* The group elected some new members before their return to Ballycarry, arriving in Belfast at a quarter past nine that evening.

1907 Local farmers approached the **Northern Counties Railway Committee** to connect up the Blackhead and Gobbins paths, but the company declined over the estimated costs of £400. NCC engineer Berkeley Deane Wise had fully intended to continue his Blackhead path on round to the Gobbins and also extend further his Gobbins Path by another three and a quarter miles north to Heddles Port, which would have involved constructing even more spectacular suspension, tubular and girder bridges and a tea house. Unfortunately, since Wise had been forced to retire through illhealth in 1906, the completing of his plans seemed to lose momentum. The NCC considered the potential construction costs of around £750, added to the annual maintenance costs of the existing Gobbins Path, about £209 per year, as too high. In **1908** only a final short extension of the path was completed, finishing near the 'Seven Sisters' caves.

1911 This Census records the **Welsh** family having moved to 9 Gransha, the tenants of farmer **Tom Browne** of Balloo townland.
Davie and Agnes Welsh had then been married for 14 years.
David Welsh 38, General Quarry Labourer
Agnes Welsh 38, wife
Nellie 12, **James** 10, **David** 8, **Agnes** 7, **Margaret** 5, **Mary** 3, **Bessie** 1 month*

1911 The **Welsh's** youngest child *****Bessie,** died aged 10 months in December this year. She is buried with her mother and father in St John's COI cemetery. **Mrs Agnes Welsh** must have had another baby a few years later, who was christened **Beatrice, 'Beattie'.** Beattie appears in 'Green Pastures'.

15 Oct 1912 The foundation stone of a new *Mullaghdubh National School* was laid by **Mrs George Smith** of *Cragoran*, Browns Bay and **Mrs WJ Porritt** of Redhall. The school, of which **Rev David Steen** was the *'esteemed manager'* and **Thomas Douther** the *'capable principal'*, had been improved and enlarged from time to time. The contractors were Douther Bros of Whitehead. The new building could accommodate about 130 scholars. A site had been obtained from **Mr Thomas Browne** and a lease from the trustees of the **Marquis of Donegall**. Rev Steen said the pupils of Mullaghdubh were now in many lands and many on the seas. A large proportion of the boys entered the Mercantile Marine and many had attained high positions bringing credit to their school. His one regret was that **Mr George Allen** of Philadelphia was not present with them. He had visited recently on his annual trip. As a past pupil he was a great credit, occupying a leading position in the commercial life of a great city on the other side of the Atlantic. Mr Allen had pledged to sent him £100 towards the building fund. Mrs Smith and Mrs Poritt were presented with a handsome solid silver trowel and bouquets. **Mr Thomas Milliken** proposed a vote of thanks. He had attended Mullaghdubh School 50 or 60 years previously and he was pleased to see his teacher then in the audience today. He of course referred to **Mr John Donaldson.** After briefly referring to several past teachers, he said they had never been better served by the present teacher **Mr Tom Douther** and his wife **Mrs Douther** as far as moral character and conduct were concerned. **Mr John Auld Duff** seconded this.

4 Aug 1914 Britain declared War on Germany. A **Home Rule Bill** had been passed but it was soon suspended and many young Ulster men went off to fight.

1915 Before the First World War, a group of Queen's University students from Belfast had rented a cottage near the Gobbins at Woodside's farm during Easter and summer holidays.They included the Belfast rugby player **Billy Edwards** and **Walter Newel** and his brothers. Locals nicknamed them 'the Pickie boys'. Maggie McBride writes about them in 'Green Pastures' . Lance Corporal Walter Newel of the Black Watch was killed in 1915. His two brothers George and David also died. A large memorial obelisk honouring Newel and his friend Captain William V. (Billy) Edwards of the Royal Dublin Fusiliers, was erected close to the Gobbins shore after the war (picture page 78). Both men had spent what Billy Edwards described as 'glorious summers' there. This monument is still there in 2014.

April 1917 A Midland Railway Company employee died suddenly at the Gobbins. **Samuel Craig,** aged 58, of Kells was part of a working party of men sent to Islandmagee each year to make necessary repairs to the Gobbins Path and bridges after winter storms. At an inquest led by the coroner **Dr Arthur Mussen**, one of Craig's fellow workman, **Robert Douglas**, gave evidence that the deceased had appeared to be in his usual health at dinner, but later as he proceeded up steps carrying his spade, he was seen to fall to the ground. Witness rushed to his assistance but Craig never spoke again. He had worked for the railway company for 9 years. Local physician **Dr Charles Dundee** of Redhall gave the cause of death as heart failure and this verdict was recorded. (from Larne Weekly Reporter)

21 Jan 1918 Second Officer **Samuel Caldwell,** aged 40, whose wife was Mary Davidson of Ballykeel, was one of 13 crew lost when *HM Transport Teelin Head*, travelling from Belfast to France with a cargo of potatoes, was torpedoed and sunk by the German submarine UC-31. Three other Islandmagee men who also perished were Chief Officer **George Ross** aged 31, whose parents were Robert and Mary Ross of Gransha , **James Duff** AB (able seaman) aged 25, son of James and Elizabeth Duff (Wilson) of Pebble Cottage and **John Jones** 34, Fireman, son of Mary Jones and the late Andrew Jones of Ballymoney townland.

28 Nov 1918 James Hill of Hill's Port at the Gobbins, aged 26, an able seaman on the **MFA Divis** attached to the Grand Fleet, died of pneumonia at Rosyth Naval Base Hospital. His parents were **John Hill** and **Margaret Mann** of Hill's Port.

17 May 1920 Edward Coey Smith of Browns Bay was putting himself forward as a candidate for the Carrickfergus division after the retirement of Colonel McNeill after 20 years. Smith had advertised in the Larne Times, *"I would ask for your wholehearted support, particularly of the rural electors,"* in the Co. Antrim elections for the County Council. (LT&WT)

2 Sept 1920 Headlines in the local LT&WT read, *'Belfast's Bloody week, twenty killed, over 200 injured, wholesale incendiarism, troops fire on mobs, curfew law enforced'.*

22 June 1921 King George V and **Queen Mary** visited Northern Ireland. The King was opening the first session of the new Northern Ireland Parliament at the Belfast City Hall. His speech, prepared by Prime Minister **David Lloyd-George**, called for an end to the war. Aircraft landed at Aldergrove, carrying cameramen and reporters who returned to London with newsreel films and photographs of the event.

April 1922 Wallpaper had arrived at 'The Gobbins Stores', Islandmagee. Proprietor **William J Hawkins** was ordering further supplies at prices from 6d per dozen. The store was described as,' *'The quality grocer and draper, Tel Whitehead 29'.*

22 April 1922 Hundreds of visitors had come to Larne and district during the good weather over Easter. Cars and charabancs were very busy on the Coast Road and at Islandmagee, with ferryboats also doing a fine trade, the Larne Times & Weekly Telegraph reported.

3 June 1922 The Minister of Home Affairs issued a curfew for the whole of Northern Ireland except Belfast. This required everyone to remain indoors between 11pm and 5am unless provided with a permit from the Royal Irish Constabulary (RIC).

June 1922 The **SS Argenta**, an old wooden steamship which was used to intern Sinn Fein sympathisers arrested during the recent conflict, was anchored in Larne Lough off the Yellow Stone near Dick's Ferry at Ballylumford until 1923. To Islandmagee locals and those imprisoned on board, it became infamous as 'The Prison Ship'.

1923 Robert (Bob) Strahan's of Gransha private bus service in Islandmagee was one of the last two in Ulster to be taken over by the NCC or Northern Counties Committee.

1924 After the death of **Mrs Agnes Welsh**, mother of Margaret McBride, 'Welsh's Tearooms' had to close. Mrs Welsh was only 52 when she died. (See also 1926).

1926 The LT&WT reported an *'exciting development'*, the grand opening of a newly refurbished **Gobbins Cafe and Tearooms** near to the Gobbins Cliffs, with Mr Brownlee's Dance Orchestra and Ballycarry Jazz Band providing entertainment. *'The antique fireplace in this apartment, which is believed to have been preserved in a practically unaltered state for a century and a half, came in for much attention. The crook, hobs, pipeboles or recesses in the jambs and low grate gave an old-time charm to the visitor'*, said the Times. It also recorded the tearooms being patronised to full capacity on Easter Monday and Tuesday that year.

1928 The building of a better road above the existing Gobbins Path began, in response to campaigning by a number of local farmers and landowners including **John Woodside**, **Tom Browne** and **Marriott Holmes**. Still referred to by older Islanders as the *'New Road,'* it took three years to complete and is today known as Gobbins Road (see picture overleaf).

May 1935 Eleven year old **Robert Woodside**, the son of **John Woodside** of Gobbins Farm, was killed after falling near the Gobbins Head while looking for seagulls eggs with his younger brother Thomas. An inquest was held

Blackhead
Lighthouse

Cove Stores

To Gobbins Path

New Road

New Road, Islandmagee. Showing Blackhead in the distance

in **Mr Kane's Tearooms** by the coroner **Dr Robert Reid JP.** The deceased lad was a pupil of Mullaghdubh Public Elementary School and was a great favourite in the district. Sadly, his would not be the last accident or tragedy at the Gobbins.

1936 Saw the death of **Thomas Browne**, who had been the Welshes' landlord.

1961 After a final repainting in 1936, the Gobbins Path had closed during the Second World War years. It remained closed until 1951, when the Ulster Transport Authority took over the repair work necessary to reopen it. But by 1954 high maintenance costs forced the UTA to abandon the project and although the path remained open for a few more years, this year it was officially closed and no longer maintained. Over the following decades the bridges and structures gradually fell into decay and became dangerous. A tribute was paid to the path in the Larne Times by Mr Douglas Dean and **Mrs Margaret McBride** wrote from her Belfast home in response to his 'fitting tribute' to the Gobbins. *"To me it has always been a path to paradise, as a child with my brothers and sisters I played often on this particular bridge, explored every cave, had a name for every bridge and knew how many steps in each stone stairway that led up to loftier heights. Often I proudly escorted tourists round the bridges and afterwards they would have a meal at my mother's teahouse where she catered for visitors for over 20 years. Now I reluctantly also must say farewell to my path of paradise with its dear familiar scenes of my childhood. But it will remain forever enshrined in my heart, where the cruel grasping sea cannot wrestle or take it from me."*

June 1965 A 10 year old Carrickfergus boy fell to his death from the Gobbins Cliffs while searching for bird's nests. The body of **Nigel Aitkin** of Sunnylands Drive was found by fisherman Patrick Smith of Ballystrudder, 25 feet below the cliff path.

Dec 1965 Mrs Margaret McBride won a Christmas turkey for the best letter to the Larne Times. She then resided at 3 Ypres Park, Whiteabbey. She wrote: *"Your request for a letter offers no difficulty, as Mr Louis Gilbert's tribute to Islandmagee in last weeks Larne Times gave me a splendid opening. Alas, I have never been a scholar, but perhaps my zeal and love for Islandmagee will surmount this difficulty. Mr Gilbert and I have traversed the same paths and found equal pleasures. I went to school with the Houston family and my father David Welsh was a close friend of Tommy Busby. The name Dixon Donaldson will be cherished by Islandmagee folk. We are a folk not apt to forget and we are proud of our seafaring men and the glorious record they have. But the grand climax was the tribute to the Gobbins, my childhood home. I have feasted on its beauty, finding the same peace and presence of God. I hope to escape away to it again when the brighter days come. I ask for no greater pleasure. Television on Islandmagee - it is unthinkable!"*

Feb 1967 Mrs Margaret McBride sent a letter to the Larne Times. *"Sir, It was sad reading about the fate of the Gobbins in your paper this week. I had been working hard for the restoration of the path and had corresponded with Mr Louis Crosby. He was sympathetic and had offered a ray of hope. I can understand the problem however, and the tremendous amount of money involved."*

1968 Margaret McBride's poem, 'Islandmagee' featured in Kilcoan schoolteacher **Victor Glenn's** re-edited and republished version of **Dixon Donaldson's** 'History of Islandmagee'.

c1972 The surviving daughters of the **Welsh** family had a reunion picture taken at the Gobbins. This included **Maggie, Aggie, Beattie** (who had come over from Australia), and **Mollie** (see Photos page 105).

1973 Hamilton B Mitchell then aged 92, was interviewed for the local paper by **David Welsh**, a son of Maggie Welsh's brother Davie and a grandson of her mother **Agnes Welsh**. Hamilton B. and his brother **Robert Hugh Mitchell** were well known blacksmiths at Loughford, Islandmagee during the early 1900s. Hamilton recalled many hack cars (hackney carriages) operating from Ballycarry Station in the summer carrying visitors to the Gobbins. *"The late Henry McNeill, who owned hotels in Larne, used to send hundreds of tourists to visit the Gobbins Path. Those same tourists were* *served with tea by your late grandmother Aggie, David, when they arrived at her tearooms there. The heavily laden hack cars used to pass by our smithy here and the passengers would wave merrily to us."*

May 1974 Margaret McBride wrote to the Larne Times. "*How pleased I was to see postcards of the Gobbins in your paper. I have the same in my possession and to me they are priceless. In later years I re-visited the scenes of my childhood and refused to pay the fee; not because I was mean but because I felt it would be an insult to me and my beloved Gobbins. My explanation had the fee-collector smiling. He bowed and bade me enter, as if I had been a princess.*" (When the Gobbins Path first opened in 1902, an all-inclusive 6d ticket brought tourists from Whitehead or Ballycarry stations by jaunting car to the top of the Gobbins Path. Islandmagee people were apparently allowed free admission to encourage local support.)

29 August 1975 When **Margaret McBride** died this year, an obituary to her was published in the Larne Times, written by **Louis Gilbert** in his 'Islander' column.

1979 The famous 'Tubular Bridge' at the Gobbins was badly damaged by gales and it finally collapsed into the sea in 1981, 80 years after it had been built.

March 1996 The death was reported of **Louis Gilbert,** well known local writer and broadcaster. Born in 1912 in Belfast, Mr Gilbert had more recently lived at Ballystrudder, Islandmagee. Having begun his career in the linen trade, he later worked for the Belfast Telegraph and was editor of the Carrickfergus Advertiser when he retired in 1977. He was particularly fond of Islandmagee and the Gobbins, and both featured in his '*Islander*' column written for the East Antrim Times and in his contributions to Walter Love's popular radio programme 'Day by Day'. Louis was survived by his wife Betty and his daughters and their families. His interment was to Islandmagee New Cemetery.

16 Aug 2009 Five climbers, 4 males and a female, were plucked to safety at the Gobbins last night during a dramatic air-sea rescue. It is understood they had been climbing on cliffs close to the Gobbins, when they became stranded. Lifeboats from Portmuck, Bangor and Larne and the Islandmagee Coastguard Cliff Rescue team were involved in the operation and a Navy rescue helicopter from HMS Gannet at Prestwick was used to winch them to safety (Belfast Telegraph).

Nov 2013 Work began on a £6 million modern restoration project of the Gobbins Marine Path, led by Larne Borough Council with European, Heritage Fund and Government funding. It is hoped to complete the ambitious project by summer 2014, bringing visitors once again to navigate the spectacular Gobbins cliffs. Plans include the reconstruction of a new clifftop path, with 15 bridges including a tubular bridge and a suspension bridge of stainless steel. A Heritage Visitor Centre with cafe and playground is also being built near Ballystrudder.

Appendix 4:

Notes

Chapter 1

1 **Berkeley Deane Wise** 1855–1909, born Co Wexford, became chief engineer of the Belfast and Northern Counties Railway Company. During his years with the company, (after 1903 was renamed the Midland Railway and Northern Counties Committee), Wise designed and managed the erection of many stations, including York Street Station, Belfast and the adjacent Northern Counties Hotel. He also developed many of the resorts visited by the railway, including Whitehead, where he was responsible for constructing the promenade, path and tearoom round BlackHead in 1892. At the Gobbins, Islandmagee he designed a scenic two mile path including staircases along the cliffs, with dramatic metal tubular and suspension bridges, caves and tunnels carved through the rock. Wise retired in 1906 through ill health, leaving plans for an extension of his path which were never fully completed. He died in 1909, it is said by his own hand.

2 Being pregnant can cause oedema or swelling in the legs as the uterus puts pressure on the blood vessels in the lower trunk of the body. It may also have indicated underlying heart problems that Agnes Welsh died of in 1924, aged only 52.

Chapter 2

1 **Edward 'Ned' Jones**, a general labourer who worked with Davie Welsh at Ballylig, was 50 and living at Mullaghdoo in 1911 with his Glaswegian wife Katey 43 and one daughter Mabel aged 13.

2 **Martha Strahan** was a daughter of **Robert Strahan** of Gransha. Strahan ran a jaunting car service to and from Ballycarry Station from the late 1800s. A son, **Bob Strahan**, also ran an Islandmagee automobile taxi and coach business in the 1920s. Robert and his wife Agnes had two grocery stores at Gransha and at Newchurch opposite St John's Church of Ireland. They stocked grocery items, hardware, confectionery, meal flour and bran. Their eldest daughters Martha and Maria were shop assistants, and Maggie Welsh tells us she was afraid to ask Martha Strahan to open the Gransha shop on a Sunday afternoon for ham and tomatoes in Chapter 6.

3 The **Holmes** family of the Gobbins were descended from a seceding Presbyterian minister, Rev William Holmes who came to preach at Islandmagee about 1767. He married a local woman, Catherine Hunter,

and settled there. The family became prosperous farmers with corn mills at the Gobbins and Millbay. By the 1900's a grandson, Edward Hunter Holmes and his family lived in 'Gobbins House' and farmed there. William 'Willie' Holmes, his elder son, became a merchant seaman. Marriott Holmes, the younger brother, farmed with their father.

4 **Hugh Dick** of Ballymoney, Islandmagee, was Schools Attendance Inspector for Islandmagee and east Antrim district from c1903-1920. This included four Islandmagee schools and those as far as Straid, Larne and Ballynure. Mr Dick visited all his schools each week by pony and trap, then a pushbike and later on he acquired a motorbike. Dick took careful notes of pupils who were regularly absent from school and then summoned their parents to attend Larne or Carrickfergus Petty Sessions court, where they could be fined several shillings plus costs. It was not uncommon for the children of Islandmagee grocers and farmers to be kept away from school to help their parents.

5 **James Kane** went to school with Maggie Welsh and unlike her, was a good artist. In 1911 he was 4 and living with his mother Mary Kane and younger brother Samuel aged 1, at the home of his grandparents, farmer Samuel Macauley, aged 70 and his wife Eliza age 60, at Mullaghdoo. We assume his father was at sea.

6 **John Macaulay**, who teased Maggie Welsh about her homemade school-bag, was born a year after her on November 24 1907 on the Kilton Lane, the eldest of six brothers. His schooling included Mullaghdubh School and then the Royal Belfast Academical Institute. His father, Captain Robert Macaulay, had been lost at sea during the First World War when his ship was sunk in the English Channel leaving his widow Margaret to bring up their six children: John, James, Robert, Ted, Norman and Cecil (twins). John later followed his father to sea, joining the well-known Head Line shipping company in 1923. His first boat, the 'Wicklow Head', was crewed almost entirely by Islandmagee men. In the late 1920s the Macaulay brothers regularly won races in local regattas in their sailing boat 'JJRENC', made up of the first initials of their names.

7 **Ballylig Limestone Quarry** – Limestone was important to people living around the shores of Larne Lough from early times. About 1796 limestone was first recorded being quarried and burnt in kilns at Ballylig, a townland above Magheramorne, about 8 miles from Islandmagee. Soon afterwards a quay was built on the nearby Magheramorne shore for schooners to carry the lime to Scotland and Wales. On Islandmagee itself, a number of local men also established thriving limestone businesses in the 1800s. The 1911 Census reported that workers at Ballylig Quarry

usually came from Gransha townland in Islandmagee and included: David Welsh, Thomas Coburn, William Stewart, Samuel McDowell, Archie Forde, William Forde and John Forde.

8 In 1927 A **'History of Islandmagee'** was published, by the well respected principal of Kilcoan Public Elementary School, Dixon Donaldson. A revised version was published by another Kilcoan school teacher, Victor Glenn, in 1968. Islandmagee Community Association republished Donaldson's original manuscript in modern format in 2002.

9 **Alfie Jackson** was one of six Islandmagee postmen in the early 1900s. The Islandmagee Post Office was then at Kilcoan and each postman had his own area.

10 The **Iron Mission Hall** in Belfast, that Maggie's elder sisters joined, was built in 1890 by evangelist preacher Charles W Lepper, off Templemore Avenue in East Belfast. These corrugated iron buildings became popular because they were very cheap to erect. More information http://www.ironhall.com/aboutus.html

Chapter 3

1 The **Caldwell** children of the Lang Dale (today Langdale) were friends with Mollie and Maggie Welsh. The death of their father Samuel in 1918, aboard the 'SS Teelin Head', is mentioned in Chapter 13

2 **John Hill** and his wife Margaret Mann lived at Hill's Port, below the Welsh's cottage at the Gobbins. They were 50 and 51 respectively in the 1901 Census. Five of their children lived with them, including Thomas a sailor aged 23, Margaret 19, a farmer's daughter, John 17, a farmer's son, Eleanor 14, a scholar, and James 10, a scholar. By the time Maggie Welsh was born the Hills had adopted an orphan girl, Annie, who later ran their tearooms as Mrs Hill was an invalid. The Hill's youngest son James, an Able Seaman on MFA Divis attached to the Naval Grand Fleet, died in November 1918 of pneumonia at Rosyth Naval Base Hospital.

3 **Mullaghdoo School** (this was the old spelling but today spelt Mullaghdubh) stands on the Middle Road, Islandmagee. A National schoolhouse was first built there in 1843. A new school building, still used in 2014, was erected close by in 1913 and further extended in 1954.

4 Maggie Welsh's teachers at Mullaghdubh(doo) school were Thomas **'Tom or Tam' Douther** and his wife **Annie**. The youngest son of John Douther of Hollow Farm, Browns Bay, Tom Douther became Principal of Mullaghdubh school in 1901. He married his assistant teacher Annie Browne, a sister of Tom Browne a Balloo farmer, who was coincidently

also the Welsh family's landlord. Annie Browne was named after her mother Annie Hill, who had also been a teacher at Kilcoan Female School in the 1850s, before marrying James Browne. A woman was expected to give up work when she married, even up until the 1960s. By a more tragic coincidence, Mrs Annie Douther died in 1924, aged only 44, the same year as Maggie Welsh's mother Agnes died at 52. Tom Douther survived his wife for another 29 years. He taught at Mullaghdubh until he retired in the 1930s. He was the last survivor of the Douther family, well known in Islandmagee and Whitehead for conducting a coal and building business. The Douther gravestone is in old Ballyprior cemetery, Islandmagee.

The Douther gravestone is in Ballyprior cemetery

5 Few tradesmen travelled into Islandmagee in the 1900s as the roads were so rough. A breadman like **Mercer** might come to a convenient point in his horse and cart and expect locals to come to him or leave their order in an arranged place.

6 **James Niblock** lived at Mullaghdoo with his mother Mary 34, and sister Agnes 8, in the 1911 census. His father is 'absent', very common in Islandmagee and was probably away at sea.

Chapter 4

1 Regattas were very popular in Islandmagee from the early 1900's. They were held annually in the summer months at Browns Bay, Millbay and Portmuck, as well as the Cove. They were very popular, attracting large crowds of holidaymakers and locals eager to participate in swimming, diving, sailing and rowing races for yachts and boats. It is believed that **Dixon Donaldson** instigated the first Cove Regatta in early 1900's and he was still involved on the organising committee up until his death in 1931. On the Cove shore was also a place for swimming known as Corcoran, with long sprung diving boards for men and ladies. The Cove Regatta was still taking place up until 1938 but it was not revived after the Second World War. The last existing Islandmagee regatta was held at Millbay up until a few years ago.

2 The Tilley Lamp, first invented by John Tilley in 1813, was used by British Army in the First World War 1914-18 and became the most popular generic name for all types of kerosene lamps. After the war the company began to produce lamps for the domestic market.

3 **Archie Forde** of Kilcoan and his sons William and John worked at Ballylig Limestone Quarry with Davie Welsh.

4 The '**Heughs**' and the '**Snabs**' were local names given to land formations along the coast stretching between the Gobbins to Cloughfin and Blackhead. 'Heughs' come from the English word for bluff, steep cliff or precipice. 'Snab', from the Irish for stub. Wee John Kane's family were known as 'Kanes of the Heughs' to distinguish them from other Islandmagee families of that name.

5 Although some people in Islandmagee would have taken the Belfast News Letter, the most popular local newspaper in the early 1900's was the **Larne Times and Weekly Telegraph (LT&WT)**. In 1937 its name was changed to Larne Times and in 1967 to the East Antrim Times.

Chapter 5

1 **Dr Charles Dundee MD, JP** of Redhall, Ballycarry, was the well-known and respected physician to the residents of Whitehead, Islandmagee and Ballycarry for over 50 years and the medical officer of the Islandmagee dispensary in 1910. He was also a dairy farmer and an enthusiastic campaigner for tenant-farmer rights. He married an Islandmagee woman, Annie Hill, a sister of Arthur Hill of Seaview and Mrs Edward Coey Smith of Browns Bay. They had two sons, Dr William and Charles. In 1934 Dr Dundee was 78 when he died after sustaining fatal injuries in a tragic accident on Ballycarry Brae, when his own car ran over him.

2 **John Auld Duff** ran a general grocery and hardware shop at what became known as Duff's Corner, Ballystrudder. Mr and Mrs John Duff and their six children lived in Causeway Villas, opposite Ballycarry Station. John Duff was remembered as a big tall grey haired man with a very florid complexion. In the 1920s he dropped dead suddenly while serving in his shop. The building is today a thriving supermarket, run by Steven Caldwell.

3 **The Rev David Steen** was ordained at First Islandmagee Presbyterian in August 1877 and served as their minister until his retirement, through illhealth, in 1928. The congregation thought so highly of him that during his career they presented him with a pony and trap and built him a large manse and a new church in 1901.

4 The Welsh's landlord **Tom Browne** was the son of farmer James Browne. By 1911, after his father's death, Tom aged 24, was farming at Balloo with his widowed mother Annie and three brothers James 27, Samuel 21 and Charles 17. His sister, Annie Browne, became Maggie Welsh's teacher Mrs Douther, see Chapter 3 above. After the Welshes left their Gobbins cottage, Tom Browne took off the thatch, raised the roof and he and his wife carried on a tearooms there. A wooden hut was built beside the cottages providing more room for the many visitors and excursionists. Mrs Browne baked and catered. When Tom Browne died in 1936, his wife continued the tearooms until the Second World War, when the Gobbins path closed to the public. Many of the same families kept coming to the Browne's holiday cottages every year until the early 1980's. They were then sold to any sitting tenants as Mrs Browne was too ill to continue.

5 The **23rd Psalm**, written by King David, comes from the Book of Psalms in the Bible's Old Testament.

The Lord is my shepherd; I shall not want. He maketh me to lie down in green pastures: he leadeth me beside the still waters. He restoreth my soul. He leadeth me in the paths of righteousness for his name's sake. Yea, though I walk through the valley of the shadow of death,
I will fear no evil: for thou art with me;
Thy rod and thy staff they comfort me.
Thou preparest a table before me in the presence of mine enemies:
Thou anointest my head with oil; my cup runneth over.
Surely goodness and mercy shall follow me all the days of my life:
And I will dwell in the house of the Lord for ever.

After the Reformation of 16th century, psalms were printed and set to music in a book known as a Psalter. They were used almost exclusively in Presbyterian congregational worship until about sixty years ago, with a 'Precentor' to start and lead the singing.The word 'psalm' is a Greek word meaning song.

Chapter 6

1 **Blackhead Lighthouse**. By May 1902 a new octagonal lighthouse had been constructed on top of Blackhead cliffs, overlooking the town of Whitehead, designed by William Tregarthen Douglass (1857-1913), Chief Engineer for the Commissioners of Irish Lights. Mr E Abernethy, a County

Antrim man appointed as the Chief Lighthouse Keeper, was transferred from Tuscar Rock lighthouse in Wexford. The lighthouse itself was 51 feet high and stood 148 feet above the high water mark. In June 1912, telephone communications were set up between the lighthouse and the nearby coastguard station. Blackhead lighthouse was originally painted red, but in August 1929 it was repainted white. In 1965 Blackhead was converted to run on electricity. Its light was then visible for 27 nautical miles. The last lighthouse keeper left Blackhead on 31 July 1975. The keepers' houses were then taken over by the Irish Landmark Trust who today offer them as holiday self-catering accommodation.

2 In 1863 the **Belfast Naturalists Field Club** was established. Every year its members travelled to places of geological, botanical and historical interest. Their first ever field trip was to Barney's Point in Islandmagee that year. The Gobbins became a favourite venue for the club to visit, especially after the new path opened in 1902 and they are recorded taking tea at Hill's Teahouse in 1903.

Chapter 7

1 **Tom Ross** was a 47 year old farmer and grocer at Gransha in 1911. His wife Annie 42, and four sons, James 19 Railway Clerk, John 17 Bank Clerk, Thomas 15 and William 12. Robert Strahan lived beside him, so may have later taken over his grocers?

2 **Rev A Wylie Blue** was minister of May Street Presbyterian Church, Belfast from 1916-1946.

3 **Billy Edwards** – One of the university boys who regularly visited the Gobbins, remembered dearly by Agnes Welsh, was Captain William Victor 'Billy' Edwards, aged 30, who was killed in action just a few days after he had assumed command of D Company the Royal Dublin Fusiliers 7th Battalion, on December 29 1917 at Deir Ibzia, Palestine and buried at the Jerusalem War Cemetery. Billy Edward's family came from Strandtown. He was a well known Irish rugby international and also an Irish swimming and water polo champion. He is also reported to have been the first man to swim Belfast Lough. The only possessions that were returned to his mother after his death included three devotional books, a cigarette case, his broken watch, whistle, pipe and pipe lighter.

One of the Belfast lads who came to stay at the Gobbins was Captain William 'Billy' Edwards, killed in 1917 during The First World War.

4 Mary Woodside married Hamilton Quee, one of a family of butchers, Hamilton Quee & Son, who had shops on the Castlereagh Road, Belfast in the early 1900s.

Chapter 8

1 Willie Holmes did indeed find 'a good woman'. He married Esther Magowan of Gransha and they had one daughter, Olive. I was unable to find a record in the newspaper of Willie Holmes's cliff painting and cannot confirm the year. Unfortunately, there are no other photos of Willie. He died on 24 April 1945 and his wife Esther in February 1983. The grave is in New Cemetery, Islandmagee.

Willie Holmes with his wife Esther Magowan and their only daughter Olive 1930s. (Photo by kind permission of their daughter, Olive Norris)

2 Miss Wilson was possibly 50 year old widow Mary Wilson, in 1911 living at Mullaghdubh on 'annuity from land and houses'.

3 Annie Shepherd Swann, **CEB.**, born Leith near Edinburgh in 1859, was a popular and prodigious writer up until her death in 1943 aged 83. Her work included romantic fiction, serials, short stores and books inspired by her involvement with both the Temperance and Suffragist movements.

4 'Beulah' was the second novel written by Augusta Jane Wilson, or Augusta Evans Wilson, (1835 -1909) the American author known as one of the pillars of Southern literature. Her nine works are: Inez (1850), Beulah (1859), Macaria (1863), St. Elmo (1866), Vashti (1869), Infelice (1875), At the Mercy of Tiberius (1887), A Speckled Bird (1902), and Devota (1907)

Chapter 9

1 Farmer **Hugh 'Hughie' Wilson** lived at Ballymuldrough townland. By 1901 he was a widower with five young children. He married again in 1910 to Margaret, a 22 year old less than half his age of 46, and by then all his children had left home. His son, **William J Wilson**, a boatswain on MFA Argus, drowned in Oct 1917 when his vessel was torpedoed on voyage to Archangel. A daughter marrried Thomas Hill of Ballykeel.

2 **William McKeen** and his brother Thomas farmed at Browns Bay and the Gobbins.

3 **Robert John 'Bob' Heddles** was friendly with the Welsh boys Jim and Davie. They went to sea with him and followed him to New York. The Heddles family lived at Gransha. In 1911 Bob's father was away 'at sea'. Mother was Agnes Heddles aged 46. Children at home were: Willie James 20, a carpenter, Agnes Jane 17, Robert John 15, Maggie Elizabeth 12 and Thomas 10.

4 **Henry 'Harry' Long**, a local farmer, was wellknown at Islandmagee concerts and soirees for his recitations. In 1911 his family lived at Gransha. Harry aged 32, was the youngest son of farmer William Long aged 82, his wife Eliza Wilson Long 75, daughter Jennie 38 and son James 34. Although William and his wife had attained 50 years of marriage, these three children, of seven living, were all unmarried.

Chapter 10
Chapter 11

Chapter 12

1 **Henry Niblock**. In 1911 Henry was 16, the son of farmer Fred W Niblock and Jane Niblock of Gransha. He had three sisters: Sarah 19, Margaret 17 and Mary 14.

2 **Robert Kane**'s family lived at Ballykeel. In 1911 William Kane was at sea. His wife Lizzie was 31. They had two sons Robert (4) and John (1). In 'Green Pastures', Lizzie Kane had just had another baby, making five boys, when she suddenly died. The children were shared out among their aunts but the eldest, Robert, who was particularly close to the Welch family, wanted to live with them.

3 **Maggie or Aggie Johnston** was a close neighbour of William and Lizzie Kane of Ballykeel. She was 63 in 1911 and her husband Robert Johnston was an unemployed mariner. They had lost two children.

Chapter 13

1 **Elizabeth Dick**, the pupil who accompanied the choir at Mullaghdubh school, was born on the Gobbins Road in 1900 to Robert Dick and Abby Fleck. The eldest of five children, she stayed on at Mullaghdubh until

she was 19 as a student teacher or monitress. Her family were members of the Methodist Church in Whitehead and every Sunday they walked there from Islandmagee to attend church, Sabbath School and a prayer meeting. She married a local, David Laird of Ballyharry. Elizabeth Laird taught in Magheramorne and Gleno schools, eventually finishing her career at Ballypriormore Primary School in Islandmagee where she retired in 1966.

2 **Samuel Caldwell** of Ballykeel, a master mariner aged 40, was second officer on the SS Teelin Head when it was sunk by mine or torpedo on voyage from Belfast to France 21 Jan 1918. He was married to Mary Davidson of Ballykeel and they had six children, Jane, Hugh, Francis, Samuel, James and Mollie. Some of these were the friends or schoolchums of the Welsh children. Three other Islandmagee men also died in this incident. (see Chapter 3)

3 **Walter Newel** was one of the 'Pickie Boys', Queen's University students from Belfast who came to stay in the early 1900's near the Gobbins in Woodside's Cottages. A number of them went off to fight in the First World War and some did not return. A memorial stone obelisk was later erected by 'their friends', near the Gobbins shore to Lance Corporal Walter Newel of the 6th Black Watch, killed in action 10 July 1915, who is buried at the old military cemetery, Wangarie, Levante. He was 26 years old. Tragically he and also his two brothers David and George Newel were all killed in the war. A Newel memorial stands in Belfast City Cemetery. Another lad remembered dearly by Agnes Welsh, was Captain William Victor 'Billy' Edwards, see Chapter 3.

Chapter 14

1 **UVF Hospital.** When the First World War began in 1914, many Ulstermen who had joined the Ulster Volunteer Force before the war, went off to fight. In 1915, James Craig, who would become the first Prime Minister of Northern Ireland, offered his father's home, 'Craigavon House', for the use of the Ulster Volunteer Force to treat their sick and wounded casualties. The UVF Hospital was officially opened on 21 July 1917. One of three that opened in Ulster, it specialised in treatment of what is today called Post Traumatic Stress Disorder. After the war the hospital was used to care for ex-servicemen.

2 **King of England.** This was fact, not just a figure of speech. After Queen Victoria's death in 1901, for the next 52 years, four male monarchs sat on the English throne until the coronation of Queen Elizabeth in 1953.

During that period reigned Edward VII 1902-1910, George V 1910-1936, Edward VIII (abdicated after one year), George VI 1936-1952.

Chapter 15

1 **Mary Teare** was Maggie Welsh's friend. They both worked as housemaids to the Smiths of Browns Bay after finishing school. In 1901, the Teare family lived at Ballydown. This included James Teare a farmer aged 50, Janet Teare his wife and seven children: William, Violet, James, John, Isabella, Kathleen and Margaret. By 1911 Isabella Teare, Mary's sister, was already a 14 year old housemaid for Charles Betram Smith at Browns Bay.

2 **Smith** family. About 1867, businessman George Smith of Carnmoney came to live at Browns Bay having purchased a large farmstead there from Malcolm McNeill of the Corran at Larne. He built a large residence named 'Cragoran', and farmed extensively. After his death, one son Charles Betram Smith, took over the farm and house while another son Edward Coey Smith, built another big house, 'Inisreen', just over the road.

3 An **Orange Hall** was built at Islandmagee in 1876 by Islandmagee LOL 1962 (see picture, page 96).

Chapter 16

Chapter 17

1 **'Wee John' Kane**, the baby that Agnes Welsh cared for so lovingly, grew up and married an Islandmagee woman, Ina Mann. They lived in Coleraine and had two sons and a daughter. As an adult he was apparently known as 'Wee Jock'.

2 **Rev Thomas R Johnston** served as minister of Greenwell Street Church, Newtownards from 1945–1974. More information from www.greenwellstreet.org/gsthistory09.pdf

3 **Tumbling Paddy**. An old farming implement, a hay collector that was harnessed to a horse. Wooden prongs gathered up the hay. When the collector was full, a chain mechanism was operated by the farmer and the hay would tumble from the rake into a mound.

Appendix 5:

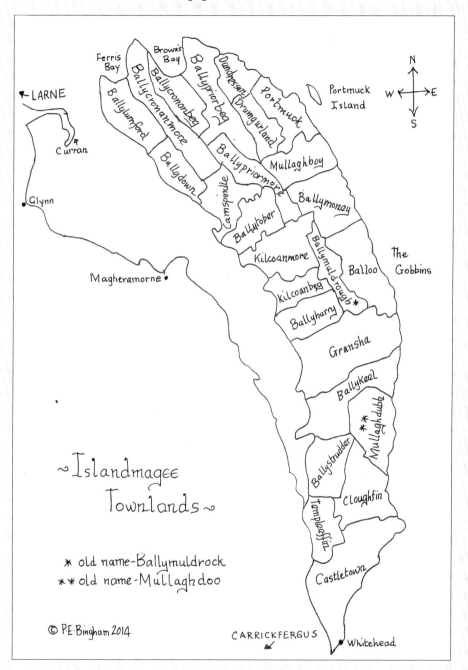

Islandmagee Townlands

Appendix 6:

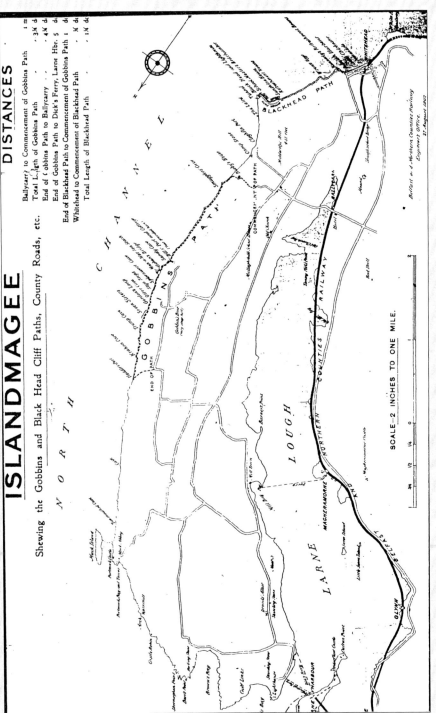

Map of Gobbins and the Gobbins Path